Butterflies *in a* Bottle

How Essential Oils Free the Emotional Self and Liberate the Body/Mind

FOURTH EDITION

Gregory T. Hitter, PhD.

The author wishes to distinguish between the word 'disease'—a concept stemming from the older scientific view that everything arises from the material, even consciousness—and the use herein of the word '*dis-ease*' describing a *lack of ease and awareness* that originates from a fragmented Self and its negative *vibrational* effects on the subtle energy body.

'*Disease*' relates to a *medical condition* diagnosed from symptoms appearing in the body or mind that are treated by implementing a palliative *therapy*.

'*Dis-ease*' relates to the results of a *fragmented* state of consciousness, conscious being, 'Self' that negatively affects the vibrational infrastructure—the 'morphogenic' (form-shaping) subtle-energy body—of an individual's system, resulting in difficulty and suffering on all levels of ones being: self-awareness (spirit), energy, mind, body, and outer life.

Dis-ease is alleviated (without diagnosis) by bringing an individual's fragmented consciousness (Self) into unity as one, whole, freely-radiant awareness, grounded in the body-mind and the present.
The SelfQuesting Approach is one such unifying method.

Fourth Edition—Revised 2009

Life Science Publishing, Lehi, UT
www.discoverlsp.com
800-336-6308

ISBN: 0-943685-58-3

About the Author

Gregory T. Hitter received his PhD in clinical psychology in 1995 from the California Graduate Institute in Los Angeles. His bachelor's degree in Physics and Math from Minnesota State University at Bemidji, MN, included the study of quantum physics and nonlinear dynamics. He integrated both disciplines in his doctoral thesis, integrating science and religion in explaining the Metaphysics of the Self, which was recognized as the outstanding PhD dissertation of the year. This booklet incorporates many of the ideas developed in that thesis and provides a theoretical explanation for the mechanism of enhanced mental and physical wellness through the vibrational energy of essential oils.

In addition to his work as a clinical psychologist, Dr. Hitter is an adjunct professor at the California Graduate Institute, and has traveled throughout the US, Europe and Asia, lecturing to scientific and medical groups. He is currently the director of the SelfQuesting Center for Whole Being in San Luis Obispo, CA.

Preface

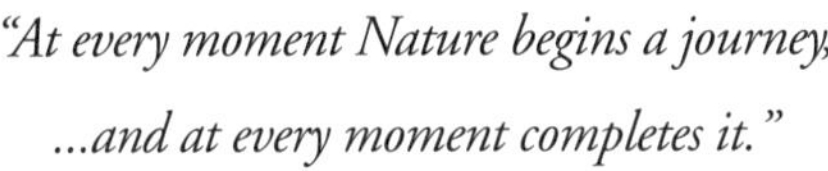

"At every moment Nature begins a journey,

...and at every moment completes it."

— Goethe —

Postmodern Enlightenment

The word 'postmodern' is used throughout this writing; it refers to a new, *enlightened paradigm* (world-view) that is developing today and is detailed here. This emerging world-view combines elements from the previous two paradigms of *science* and *religion* into "a whole that is greater than the sum of its parts." Yet the postmodern *enlightened paradigm* is much more than merely a synthesis or 'marriage' of religion and science.

Instead, the postmodern paradigm is entirely a newborn *child,* created from their bond, which fully reconciles the differences and limitations of science and religion as we have typically known them to be. It accomplishes this reconciliation not simply through a synergy of shared ideas, but rather by aiding us to *overcome the divisions within us*—the fragmenting of our individual awareness. So that from this new wholeness of conscious being, OneSelf, can come a wellness, meaning, and abundance that has been all too commonly absent from human history.

The postmodern is therefore necessarily a *consciousness-based* paradigm; it is 'enlightened' by the light of our consciousness in its wholeness, a unity in and of "OneSelf." In this, the postmodern ultimately comes to acknowledge the *four-fold levels of reality*—consciousness, energy, mind, and the physical—and to understand the causal *reign* of consciousness over the 'lower' three levels, and thus the profound, but simple and practical wisdom of "as above, so below" and "as within, so without," as well as the deep drive and need to have OneSelf. The *enlightened paradigm* acknowledges the subtle but powerful role—the "butterfly effect"—of subtle energy or "vibration" in this hierarchy.

The Vibe of Essential Oils

"As above, so below" is a perennial truth noting how consciousness directs *subtle energy,* a life-force vibration, that serves as the infrastructure of our mind, body, and life in the material world. Many of the scientific discoveries of the last century—particularly *quantum physics* and *Chaos science*—confirm this ancient, consciousness-based view, as the reflections of Niels Bohr, Albert Einstein, Werner Heisenberg, David Bohm, and others elaborated. Thus, out of classical modern science (physics) was born "postmodern" scientific thought, as an acknowledgement of the import of consciousness and subtle energy in the scheme of things.

So it's no great surprise to find ourselves at the dawn of the 21st century trying to deepen our understanding of the nature of subtle energy and this *new field* called "vibrational medicine," as well as the myriad forms of vibrational tools coming available daily.

Of the vibrational tools presenting today, perhaps the most multi-modal, powerful, complex, and yet at the same time elegantly simple, are those formed by the hand of the Creator working through Nature's abundantly diverse plant kingdom. Here in *essential oils*, the lifeblood of plants, we find the Life-force vibrationally reflected in its *most concentrated* form (except perhaps in *human consciousness* that is). For those who dare to be open to this new frontier, who allow themselves to experience the depth of Beauty that essential oils offer, a wondrous journey into a "brave new world" awaits!

But beware, a plant oil ought not be considered "essential" until <u>proven</u> worthy! And the only way to fully prove an oil's quality is by *gas chromatography / mass spectroscopy / nuclear magnetic resonance* undertaken in a multi-stage analysis. Without this analysis it's unknown whether you have a *true essential oil* or one of the plethora of pretenders that glut the market today. Both the presence of proper constituents (to *ISO AFNOR therapeutic-grade* standards and beyond) and the absence of impurities should be confirmed before a plant oil is considered fit to be relied on as "essential."

The journey into essential oils is one of *relationship*. Once an oil is *proven essential,* as noted above, one can confidently then begin to develop a relationship with it, and *trust* it will be *true*. With this in mind, enjoy your journey into the amazing world of essential oils.

To the heretics, who seek the Truth with all their heart and being, and so compel a transformation, to Beauty.

Contents

"Behold the Butterfly of Omnipotence! Its wings etched with stars and moons and suns! The soul expanded into Spirit… alone in the region of lightless light, darkless dark, thoughtless thought, intoxicated with its ecstasy of joy in God's dream of cosmic creation."

—Sri Yukteswar (beloved master of Paramahansa Yogananda)—

1

The Enlightened Postmodern World!

"The path of science is strewn, like an ancient desert trail, with the skeletons of discarded theories that once seemed to possess eternal life."

— Arthur Koestler —

Introducing the Enlightened Postmodern World-View

The use of essential oils, in everyday healing practices and in the sacred rituals of nearly all religions, dates back to the most distant reaches of antiquity. Essential oils such as frankincense and sandalwood have ancient traditions of use for healing, initiation, meditation, invocation, and altering awareness, while other oils like juniper and cedarwood have also long been used for balancing and cleansing, creating a sacred space, and even "casting out" demons. Recent clinical studies have confirmed the ability of essential oils, such as frankincense, to positively alter the RNA and DNA of our body's cells, and to penetrate the blood-brain barrier—which speaks to the potential of essential oils to powerfully affect the mind and body, and to heal chronic "dis-ease" of all varieties, even cancer (more in *Chapter 2*).

But *how* are essential oils able to bring about such dramatic changes in the body/mind? To understand the ability of essential oils to produce this wide range of powerful effects, we must first understand them in the light of an *expanded* view of reality and human being. This expanded view must account for powerful but subtle, determining influences that typically have gone unacknowledged in the Modern Age.

A New Enlightened Wholism

One such expanded view of reality is currently developing and taking root as an *alternative* to the two previous great world-views of *pre-modern religion* and *modern science*. This emerging alternative world-view is called the "postmodern" or *enlightened paradigm.* Though this new vision of reality incorporates understanding from both former world-views, it is not merely a bridging or merging of the material reasoning of modern science with the enduring ancient wisdom of religion, but entirely *a new vision.* This new paradigm offers a renewed way of being, and a way of knowing, by which we are able to understand, acknowledge, and empower ourselves in ways never before possible.

In particular, *postmodern science*, as it developed out of quantum physics, has given *scientific* understanding of the need to expand our vision of reality, by confirming the existence and the importance of *subtle fields of energy* that exist in and around us and powerfully influence the material world, determining its expression. More importantly, this new vision has confirmed the interplay of this subtle energy with our *consciousness,* thus acknowledging even subtler and more profound levels of our being-ness, as well as awakening us to our intimate connection with our world, and the cosmos.

In so doing, this enlightened, postmodern science has enhanced and grounded our understanding of the enduring wisdom within religion and its views of the relationship between subtle energy (prana, chi, life-force, tao, implicate order, etc.) and our consciousness or self-aware being (spirit, soul, Self, sentience, etc.). ***This new recognition of subtle, 'butterfly' levels of reality allows us to see how consciousness and intent—specifically our own conscious, self-aware being, or 'Self'—is able to structure subtle, living energy fields in our system which lead us toward dis-ease or well being.***

"The same organizing forces, that have created Nature in all its forms, are responsible for the structure of our soul, and likewise for our capacity to think."

—Werner Heisenberg, Physics and Philosophy—

The Butterfly Effect

One new, but well-known concept called the "***butterfly effect,***" specifically speaks to the power of subtle influences in noting how "a butterfly flapping its wings in Brazil can cause a tornado in Texas" (E. Lorenz, *Predictability: Can the Flap of a Butterfly's Wings in Brazil Cause a Tornado in Texas?,* Address to the Annual Meeting of the *American Association for the Advancement of Science*, 29 December 1979; see *Chaos: The Making of a New Science* by James Gleick for details of this discovery).

Applying this new concept of the *butterfly effect* awakens us to the significant role that consciousness plays, as a subtle but powerful influence, in creating and directing the "morphogenic" (form-shaping) energy fields that determine the structure and expression of living systems. In this, the butterfly effect provides a conceptual understanding of how consciousness can *structure the energy* of dis-ease or wellness into our body/mind. ***Likewise, the subtle vibrational life-force provided by Nature in essential oils profoundly affects living systems. Comprehending essential oils as vibrational tools that can alter the energies of living systems is the first step toward understanding their properties and limits, and thus to knowing how they can be best applied toward whole-being at all levels.***

This new respect for the subtle power of consciousness—our conscious, sentient (self-aware) being or "Self"—has also given new meaning to the language of *religion,* and its use of words like 'soul' and 'spirit.' It shows where religion might have detached from the ground of reality, and taken flight into a vague mysticism, or fallen into the darkness of dogma, politics, and superstition.

The dogma, prejudice, and superstition of *modern science* have likewise been exposed by this new *consciousness-based* scientific paradigm, as it demonstrates how modern science has set limits on itself and its vision, in science's tendency to *reduce* its grasp on reality to measuring, predicting, and controlling the material world (reductionism).

The marriage of the pre-modern, right-brained paradigm of faith and religion with the modern, left-brained paradigm of science has resulted in the birth of a new, whole-brained, enlightened child that is wholly revolutionary—a new, enlightened, "postmodern" world-view that sees human realities from a higher ground, free from the limits of either of the two previous world-views—a different way of thinking, feeling, and being, and a more profound way of belonging and acting in the world.

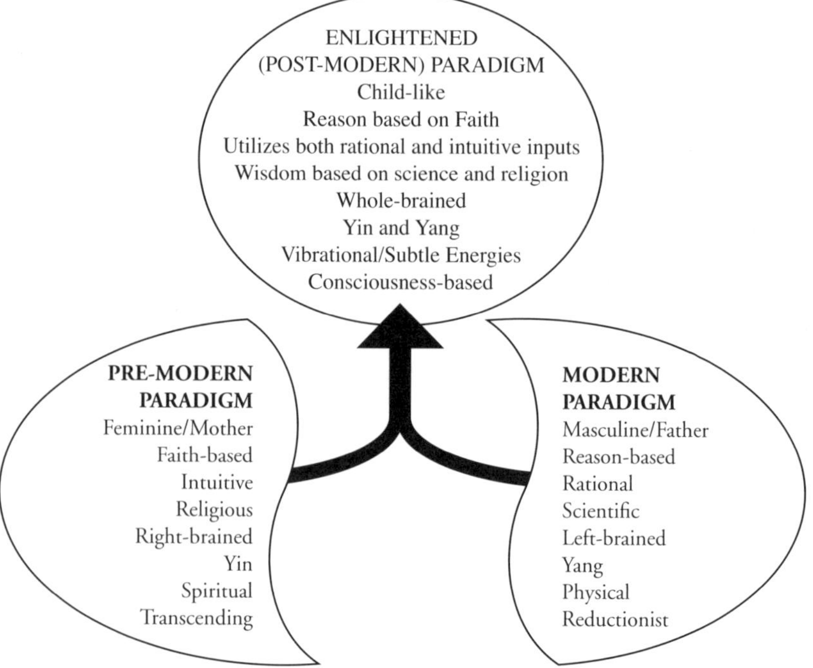

On the importance of this union, the renowned physicist Albert Einstein noted, *"Science without religion is blind; religion without science is lame."* Religious figures, like Thomas Aquinas, also recognized the need for this union of opposites, religion and science ("yin/yang" as the Taoist would put it), in attempting to unite reason with faith. This union of the *masculine principle* (our rational, scientific nature) and the *feminine principle* (our supra-rational, intuitive nature) importantly produces "a whole that is greater than the sum of its parts"—a more self-realized whole, propelling individuals into a new enlightened synergy evolving into the "postmodern" world.

The Structure of Dis-ease

The ability of essential oils to produce a physical/chemical positive effect on the human system by imparting oxygen and other molecules is relatively well known. Yet to stop at this mere *physical basis* for understanding and applying essential oils is to limit ourselves to an *incomplete vision*—the myth of modern classical science—which has focused on measuring and controlling the physical world, has limited our view of *how* reality works (to being a material *machine*), and has contributed to our inability to see important *subtler influences.* This *mechanistic reductionism* has set serious limits on both our understanding of our potential, as well as the potential of "vibrational" tools such as essential oils.

Likewise, the ability of essential oils to produce an expanding effect on human consciousness or "spirit," has been acknowledged in religious practices for millennia, and has been documented in the ancient, sacred texts of most of the world's religions, to include several hundred references to essential oils in the Christian Bible (see also the Vedic, Egyptian, and the earlier Sumerian writings). But we need not limit our understanding of oils (or ourselves) to the often-vague mysticism or dogmatic understanding of most present or ancient spiritual practice. ***Nor need we limit ourselves to an eclectic synthesis (a hybrid) of these two apparently conflicting views (religion and science), as is common today.***

Quantum physics, a critical contribution to postmodern scientific thought, has taught us how modern science's "classical" notions of the physical world are incomplete, and that *material-based* laws (by which some believe they can fully understand the world and its causes) are themselves subject, like all matter is, to the *quantum* and sub-quantum world of subtle energy and its laws. As many leading researchers in the new physics (Einstein, Bohr, Heisenberg, Bohm) have indicated, these quantum and sub-quantum realms of subtle energy, that include the *morphogenic ('form shaping') energy fields* of the human system, are subject to an even a deeper influence, that of human *consciousness, faith and intent.* Thus, the subtle energy fields of all living systems are themselves subject to even more fundamental laws that are a little "closer to home," because they bring our own individual consciousness, or 'Self,' into play.

> *"All my attempts to adopt the theoretical foundations of physics [to new quantum knowns] failed completely. It was as if the ground had been pulled out from under one, with no firm foundation on which a new physics could be built."*
>
> —Albert Einstein—

Vibrational Quality Control

So to truly comprehend the effects of *essential oils* we must understand and consider their subtle *vibrational qualities* (frequency, energy, waveform, "light") as they are uniquely shaped within Nature. Then we must appreciate the ability of the vibrational fields of essential oils to affect the energy forms that underlie and direct the human system, and 'heal' (or make *whole* - the root word of 'heal'). One can then begin to also understand the *limits* of essential oils to heal, in terms of their ability or inability to stimulate a *permanent* change in the structure of one's consciousness (a major determinant of our energy fields), and thereby effect a change at *the fundamental level* of our being, the Self, and so contribute to enduring wellness. (A good overview & introduction to the ability of vibrational tools to affect the body/mind is the book *Vibrational Medicine* by Richard Gerber, MD.)

From the above we can also see why chemists in a laboratory face difficulty trying to *synthetically* create an effective, *therapeutic-grade* essential oil. *Modern* science is very much focused on the *physical* interaction of elements, compounds, and their environment (chemistry) and does not fully or appropriately consider the subtle *vibrational* influences that compose the energy levels of reality—much less the even more powerful effects of consciousness (spirit) on living energy fields.

When one considers the role of *consciousness* in determining life-force and energy fields, then one begins to understand how attempting to create a vibrational tool such as an essential oil might be better suited to the *alchemist*, who is more familiar with the effects on subtle energy created by the 'leaded' fear of the insecure ego (fragmented [*structured*] consciousness), and how to transmute (un-structure) the *lead* of the ego into the freely-radiant *gold* of the unified Self. Modern science, with its smug self-appreciation that tends to devalue or ignore everything outside its limited reach, will not likely come to grasp the import of the symbolic, allegorical, or practical implications for human consciousness (or its influences on subtle energy and healing) that lie in alchemy's desire to "transmute lead to gold."

"Until man duplicates a blade of grass, Nature can laugh at his so-called 'scientific' knowledge. Remedies from chemicals will never stand in favor compared with the products of Nature, the living cell of the plant, the final result of the rays of the Sun, the Mother of all life."

—Thomas Edison—

In bringing the *vibrational* subtleties of essential oils into consideration, one comes to appreciate the importance of the proper growing, handling, manufacturing, and distribution of essential oils – the quality of which processes are crucial to providing truly "therapeutic-grade" oils that are capable of creating the desired effect. Understanding the quality-control needs of processing essential oils from aromatic plants must necessarily go well beyond just testing the subtle balance of the delicate energy fields, the living "life-force," that Nature has placed in the oil, the *life-blood* of the plant.

In light of the effects of consciousness on morphogenic energy fields (more later), and in regard to preserving and using these subtle energy fields that Nature has placed in the oils of plants, it would no doubt also be wise to consider the effect of the *consciousness* of those involved in growing, making, and distributing when choosing a *brand* of essential oils, as well as the effect of *one's own awareness and intent* when applying an essential oil.

Still, a *crucial* initial determinant of a product's fitness to be an essential oil would have to be a confirming analysis such as *gas chromatograph* (GC) or *mass spectroscopy* (MS). One company, *Young Living Essential Oils*, involves all its oils within a multi-stage analysis that includes GC/MS (or NMR), thus verifying its fitness to truly be called and used as a therapeutic *essential* oil (more later).

So the reductionism of modern science is self-limiting and prejudiced, because it prevents consideration of the deeper effects of consciousness to create and direct living fields of energy, which in turn determine the state of an individual's mind, body, and life. Attempting to apply old scientific views and methods to try to act on ever-more-subtle *physical* levels of energy alone, will not likely produce a satisfactory grasp of the vibrational nature of essential oils and their interplay with consciousness and the body-mind. Consciousness and the living vibrational level simply cannot be understood or harnessed by modern science's machine-like focus on measuring the material or breaking it down into parts. Perhaps a new, more comprehensive science should be defined—a *subjective science of consciousness (Goethe)*—that better appreciates this interplay of our conscious being (Self) with subtle energy and, through that, with the mind and body.

Regardless of what one thinks of modern science and religion, if one is to understand the power of essential oils and how to apply them optimally, one must reach beyond modern science and religion *to an experience of the Self,* in coming to understand the power of vibrational tools and human consciousness to influence the body/mind.

"Twenty-first century health care will be based upon the subtle energy principles and interventions involving the mind, body, environmental, and spiritual dimensions."

—Kenneth R. Pelletier, Ph.D., UCSF School of Medicine
(Author of Mind as Healer, Mind as Slayer)—

"For [over forty] years now there has been a slow shift in the paradigm of healing from the monotheism of scientific medicine"

—C. Norman Shealy, MD, Ph.D.
(founding president, American Holistic Medical Association)

SUMMARY: TWO GREAT WORLD-VIEWS BECOME ONE

The Pre–Modern Paradigm: the right-brained, supra-rational, faith-based, "feminine" (yin), religious world-view that places its focus on the non-physical world. This religious paradigm generally sees the body as at least difficult and to be transcended, if not downright "sinful" and to be rejected outright. In this, the religious world-view tends to alienate "spirit" (consciousness) from the body by devaluing the physical (the body and the world). The politically-minded followers of the pre-modern world-view felt threatened enough by different religious views and modern science, which led them to become political and even persecute, imprison, and kill those who held discordant beliefs.

The Modern Paradigm: The left-brained, rational, reason-based, "masculine" (yang), scientific world-view that focuses its action and theory on measuring, predicting, and controlling the *physical* world —without giving attention to any other reality, ignoring what it could not measure, and even devaluing as "unreal" that which could not be measured. In this *reducing* of reality (reductionism) to only what can be measured (the physical), the modern scientific world-view devalues consciousness, furthering its separation from the body. Under the scientific paradigm one generally comes to "know" by breaking everything down into its smallest parts (as if it were a machine), thus in general believing "the whole is equal only to the sum of its parts." In this, the modern scientific paradigm alienates one from Nature, including one's own true nature (Self), and creates a view of life as a cold, meaningless, material-focused existence with *nothingness* both before birth and after death.

As with religion, the politics of modern science persecutes those who don't hold accepted beliefs and methods. This is particularly evident, for example, in the rise and dominance of allopathic medicine in the 20th Century. Its political positioning resulted in the legal persecution of those who practiced outside its stringent guidelines and controls.

Because the modern and pre-modern views are incomplete, but used 'as if' complete, adopting one view drives us ultimately to the other in an attempt to avoid an inherent resulting imbalance. But even the synthesis (joining) of these two views has resulted in a dichotomy (split) and sense of alienation within the contemporary individual and culture—a state of division and dis-ease—rather than our rightful heritage of unity, empowerment, and well-being (whole being).

The Enlightened (Postmodern) Paradigm: Beyond an "eclectic" synthesis of the modern and pre-modern, the emerging enlightened world-view is a new *child*—a whole unto itself that is *greater* than simply the marriage of these previous two paradigms, and thus *greater than the sum of its parts.* This synergistic world-view heralds a union of the individual's Self with the Cosmos. It is a new way of thinking, feeling, and being that transcends and moves to overcome the alienation of the modern individual and society. The enlightened paradigm is the natural evolution of the human "spirit" (consciousness) and its *reunion* with itself, to be fully grounded in the body/mind and the world. This world-view *transcends, yet integrates* the polarities of yin-yang, rational and intuitive, science and religion into a united *whole-brain* Being (Self).

One hallmark of the enlightened view, "the whole is greater than the sum of the parts." recognizes the subtle, but powerful *butterfly effect* of consciousness (Self) and its subtle energy (vibration) in determining what occurs in the body, mind, and life. This oneness leads to a more *correct* sense of not only what is required to ground individual consciousness into *wholeness* in the body, but how to create true well-being in the individual—and, from that, the world.

Another major difference lies in the postmodern paradigm's focus on the *individual,* and *then* from that to the society that enlightened individuals create. Because truly Self-realized individuals are less alienated from their awareness and body (and thus not suffering in a way that causes them to feel alienated from the rest of the world), no longer is war, injustice, and poverty tolerated. Enlightened, postmodern individuals are not as given to casually accept or turn away from suffering or injustice as before–knowing the undiscovered potential that exists cocooned within each individual and all of humanity. They realize through a profound connectedness within (and from that with the world) that if anyone suffers, then each of us suffers and peace is not possible.

Thus, each individual's complete Christed Being, Self, or wholeness (of consciousness and "conscious being") is allowed full realization under the new, enlightened world-view. This *way of knowing,* and act of coming home to Self, *is* the enlightened world-view that is being born today from the limitation and chaos created in the failure and breakdown of the previous two world-views to provide the needed wholeness.

The *whole-brained functioning* associated with this way of being is very much supported by the vibrational qualities of *essential oils* and the life-force placed therein by the Creating Consciousness acting in Nature. Thus, proper implementation of essential oils (aromatherapy) *necessarily* involves an intuitive, whole-brained approach that appreciates the vibrational nature of oils under the directive influence of consciousness. Such an implementation goes well beyond a *knowing* gathered from classes or any previous experience of essential oils. When done with integrity, essential oil use involves a *presence and intuition* far beyond that typical of the practitioners of the previous two paradigms, and involves a stepping into one's own God-beingness as a Self-filled state of grace that is absent of selfishness and narcissism.

[*Note*: By implementing a consciousness-based world-view, where *consciousness* is seen as the driving and directing force behind everything, one method, called *the SelfQuesting Approach*™ for creating whole states of consciousness, empowers one to understand and implement a process that goes to the deepest cause of why any issue manifests, and reunites the Self from its fragmented elements. In this, *SelfQuesting*™ is a truly enlightened approach (for more see www.selfquesting.com), involving the use of essential oils to support whole being and wholeness of consciousness into the body, mind, and life as total well-being. More will be shared on this method in coming pages.]

2

Illuminating DNA cell memory with the light of consciousness

"A curse causeless shall not come."

— Proverbs 26:2—

Clinical Studies on Fragmented Consciousness

Numerous clinical studies over the last fifty years have dramatized for the medical community the link between mind and body, contributing to the appearance of branches of medicine such as *psychoneuroimmunoendocrinology*, which, as its name implies, focuses on the interplay between the psyche, the nervous system, the immune system, and the endocrine system, and their further effects on the body (for more, see *Who Gets Sick,* by Blair Justice, MD, 1987). But these studies also indicate something much deeper than merely a connection of the nervous, immune, and endocrine systems with the *mind's* thoughts, emotions, and imagery. The findings hint at a deeper, more causal level of our being—*that of our consciousness*—in determining *how* we get sick.

One insightful study, demonstrating the role of consciousness in determining what happens in our body/mind, was carried out by a team of medical doctors and written about in *A Remarkable Recovery* (Barasch & Hirshberg, 1995). This medical study (see also Hall, N.R.S. *et al*, 1994, *Advances*: 10,7-15) hinted at realities far beyond the incomplete, material-based, scientific 'rules' of modern medicine and *psychoneuroimmunoendocrinology*. It powerfully and conclusively demonstrated the *direct* role of consciousness in structuring dis-ease.

The study focused on certain people suffering from what was then called "Multiple Personality Disorder" (later labeled "Dissociative Disorder"), and how entirely differing diseases can appear in the *same* person depending on the so-called "personality" (state of consciousness or fragment of Self) presenting at the time. For example, one person studied showed the clinical symptoms of diabetes in one personality (state of consciousness), which required insulin to keep them healthy. When another personality (fragment of Self) presented, this same person showed none of the symptoms of diabetes, but had a *cardiac* condition instead, requiring heart medication to sustain them. While in yet another personality (state of consciousness), this same person showed *no symptoms* of disease whatsoever. Keep in mind these are *medical doctors* doing this study who are well-versed in medical diagnosis!

What this study indicates is the power of consciousness, our *splintered* Self or many *selves*, to structure dis-ease or wellness into our body/mind. Not all of us have this *lack* of a sentient *core* or "ego" giving some appearance of uniform self—as is seen with those diagnosed with a dissociative disorder—that would cause fragments of Self to appear as distinct states of consciousness or "personalities," each with differing expressions in the body/mind. Dynamic psychology has long recognized that we *all* fragment and undergo what psychologists and psychiatrists call "schizoid splitting." ***The extent and kind of our fragmentation (or wholeness) determines the appearance and structure of "dis-ease" (or well being) in our body/mind, as well as its "co-incident" (synchronous) appearance in our outer environment.***

Because this interplay exists between the body, the mind, the subtle energy, and consciousness, symptoms of dis-ease can often be read like a *metaphor*, giving one a clue about the nature of the fragmented consciousness that lies behind the symptoms. ***The patterning of this underlying Nature can also give clues as to the essential oils that might be useful in releasing***

the trapped or blocked consciousness and healing the body-mind-energy that it directs. Understanding these tell-tale "patterns of similarity" (metaphors)—that relate essential oils, dis-ease, and consciousness to each other—can be a valuable aid in discovering and uniting the awareness and energy of the Self, and then integrating this new wholeness into *truly holistic* well-being in the body-mind and life of the individual.

The findings of this clinical study on multiple personality (dissociation) present a fundamental challenge to modern science and medicine's *material-based* view of reality that cannot adequately describe "dis-ease" with over-simplified *physical* explanations of the mind's link to the nervous, endocrine, and immune systems, even considering hyper-intellectual concepts involving the interplay of the nervous and hormonal systems, such as "neural nets". Because of a dependency on reductionist views, modern medicine and psychiatry are seriously hamstrung by a limited understanding of the fundamentals involved and how dis-ease needs to be approached in terms of *un-structuring* the fragmented Self and creating fundamental wholeness toward whole well-being.

DNA and Energy Vibration: The Light Linking Consciousness with the Body-Mind

Other recent research has also demonstrated the connection between our consciousness, subtle-energy fields, and our body/mind. The ability of subtle vibrational fields of energy to directly affect the patterning of DNA was noted by scientists (V. Poponin, *The DNA Fantom Effect: Direct Measurement of a New Field in the Vacuum Substructure*; D. Winter, *Alphabet of the Heart: The Genesis in Principle of Language and Feeling)*. What this research reported was that subtle electro-magnetic fields in and around the body ("light" or subtle vibrational energy) determine which nucleic acids are allowed to attach to the DNA nucleic-acid receptor sites that form the amino-acid links between the twisted-pair strands of DNA (like rungs on a twisted ladder). In this way, subtle vibrational energy determines *DNA/RNA structure* and genome expression.

DNA, sometimes referred to as "cell memory," serves as a template for RNA production, thus determining in what manner RNA then directs the production of powerful, complex cellular proteins (glycoproteins) that act as the *body's messengers.* These body messengers include *neuropeptides* such as hormones, endorphins, neurotransmitters, and other potent cellular proteins that serve as powerful, cascading signals to the body and biochemically influence what happens in us physically and mentally. What is also of interest, here and in the findings of many other studies involved in recording the subtle energy fields of living systems, is the measurable effect that the *consciousness* of the subject and observer (and vibrational tools such as essential oils!) have on an individual's vibrational fields and their DNA.

Another researcher, endocrinologist Candice Pert (1997) in her book *Molecules of Emotion* described her years of research at the National Institute of Health, initially studying the connection between our mind and immune system, which later extended to the effects of consciousness on the body/mind as a whole. Dr. Pert noted how our cellular biochemistry radically shifts *instantaneously*, at the level of DNA and RNA, with the appearance of a thought, emotion, belief, or *any shift of consciousness.* From her studies, it seems that we exist in a subtle energy field ('aura' or 'prana') in which any shift of awareness instantaneously causes this concurrent shift in the vibrational infrastructure to imprint DNA and direct the *manifestation* of complex cellular proteins (glycoproteins—specifically *neuropeptides*) in every living cell of the body. These complex proteins or *body messengers* then cascade to profoundly affect our entire system, signaling throughout the body/mind to influence its relative state of well-being or dis-ease.

Thus a pathway is suggested for how consciousness and its influence on morphogenic (form-shaping) vibrational fields can influence the physical, by specifically determining the structure of DNA/RNA *cell memory*, and thus affect cellular biochemistry and *structure* dis-ease or wellness into the body/mind.

Consciousness and Energy: The Source of the Body's Knowing

Of special interest in terms of *essential oils* are the results of medical research in Tubingen, Germany (Glaser et al, 1999, "Boswellic acids and malignant glioma: Induction of apoptosis but no modulation of drug sensitivity," *British Journal of Cancer*). Using DNA end-labeling and electron microscopy, these researchers noted how the boswellic acids from frankincense ("boswellia") were able at very low micro-molar concentrations to affect the DNA of the cells of laboratory mammals and cause *cancer cell death* or apoptosis. Furthermore, they noted that the action of frankincense in doing this did not appear to conflict with or otherwise inhibit cancer chemotherapy treatment, nor did it require RNA synthesis for proteins, nor did it cause free-radical formation, nor was it blocked by free radical scavengers—suggesting an unknown *independent pathway of cause and effect,* such as a more direct vibrational method, rather than merely a biochemical one.

What is being noted in this Tubingen (Germany) University Medical School study is that the presence of frankincense (boswellia) caused an *anti-cancerous* effect that had little to do with its interference with any *particular* step in the commonly understood and accepted pathway of cellular biochemistry: 1. DNA templates RNA; 2. RNA determines the production of cellular proteins [neuropeptides] in the organelles of the cell; 3. Cellular proteins are then released into and out of the cell to affect the body and mind.

Instead, because "no RNA protein synthesis was required" and "no free radicals were formed" suggesting no pre-cell-death chemical processes that created or were blocked by free radicals, we are left with the suggestion of *a more direct, vibrational effect on DNA* resulting in cancer cell death. Said in another way, the *wholistic* vibrational (rather than chemical) quality of frankincense transcended and altered the *dis-ease* (the cancer cells), vibrationally.

This brings us back to the previously noted research pointing to the ability of subtle energy or "light" (such as the vibrational quality of essential oils) to directly affect the nucleic acid links of DNA twisted-pairs. In the cancer study on mammals done with boswellia (frankincense) the change in DNA resulted in cancer-cell death. It should be noted that alternative medicine has long acknowledged the powerful antitumor effect of frankincense and other essential oils.

This research into the physics and biochemistry of our body's cells and their DNA has shown how subtle energy affects the DNA and RNA, that in turn can determine the biochemistry and what happens in every cell, tissue, and organ in our body. This sheds light on how the morphogenic, subtle-energy fields of consciousness and vibrational tools such as essential oils are able to influence and heal.

We can also consider the chemical research on other essential oil compounds such as *d-limonene*—present in oils like frankincense, pine, and citrus oils—and d-limonene's known effect in repairing DNA/RNA. Dozens of studies have shown that d-limonene has a chemical anti-cancer effect. Yet, as previously mentioned here, this research struggles to adequately describe the full action of these oils in killing cancer cells. We must look beyond modern objective science and also apply an *expanded subjective science* in beginning to grasp the total effect of vibrational tools such as essential oils and the powerful *life-force* placed in them through the action of Nature, the hand of the Creator.

DNA/RNA Patterning (Cell Memory and Vibrational Energy: the link between consciousness, essential oils, and the body/mind)

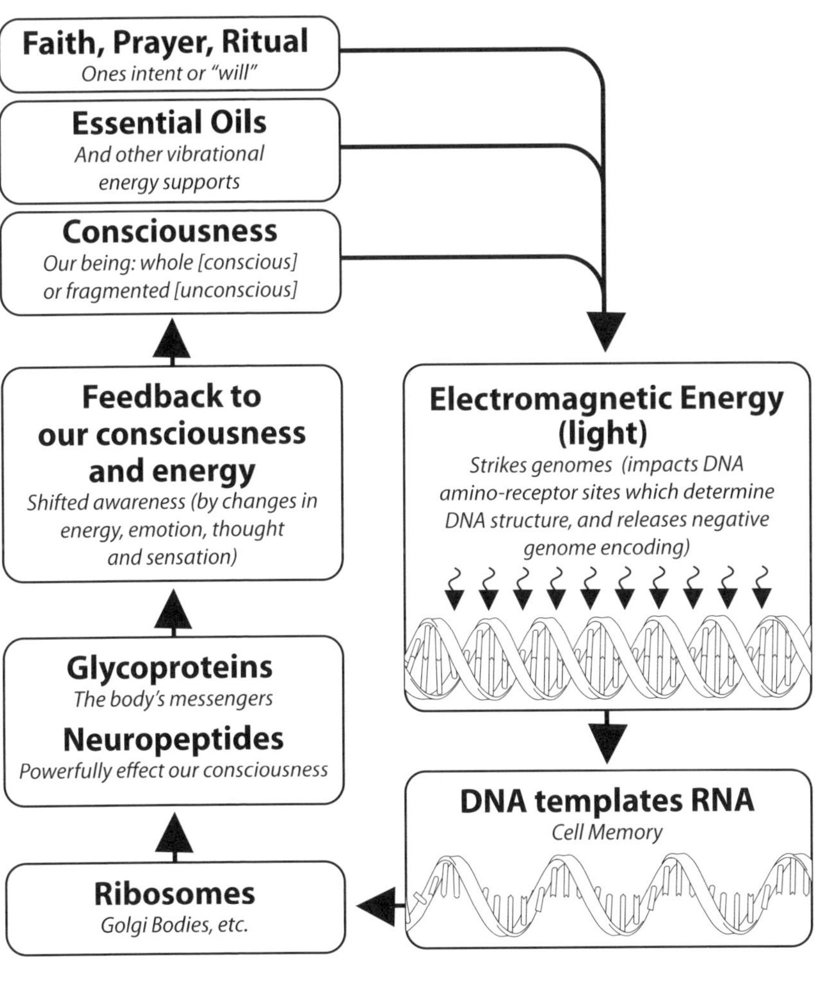

When one repeatedly witnesses these therapeutic effects through clinical practice, one soon realizes that a controlled, multi-million-dollar FDA-sanctioned study isn't necessary (much less *able*) to confirm the influences of consciousness and vibration on the physical.

To understand the *reasoning* behind what is being said here is *one* way of grasping the potential of essential oils. But when one, with an open mind, observes an essential oil *still in the bottle* positively influence the physiology and psychology of a person merely by being placed near their body (within their energy field, without the person seeing it placed there), or by being placed on or near someone with whom they are energetically connected or presently communicating by phone (again, without the person's knowledge), then one gains a deeper respect for the vibrational character of essential oils.

Though research has verified the vibrational effect of essential oils, to *see* it happen can greatly open one to its wonder and potential—provided one's make-up allows one to accept the experience into their world-view and not turn away. The renowned physicist Max Planck commented regarding the inability of those holding one world-view to traverse the revolutionary divide to a different geometry (to paradigm shift from classical to quantum physics), "Old physicists don't change their mind; they die, and new physicists come along who don't have the old problems." ***Proper and comprehensive use of essential oils requires a faith in action—shaped by experience and whole being—and the ability to be and move forward in the unknown. Too often practitioners of science and religion do not possess or exhibit the personal dynamics allowing for the openness required for good-faith use of essential oils. Their results are thus programmed to fail, as confined by their fragmented Self and its world-view, which limits their expectations and prevents the free-flowing interplay of the proper intuition, awe, and wonder, not to mention vibration, 'will' and 'intent'.***

3

Unifying the self: changing the infrastructure of dis-ease

"We arrive at the truth not by reason alone, but also by the heart."

— Blaise Pascal—

So, by understanding the role that subtle energy and consciousness play in creating dis-ease or health in the body/mind, one can begin to comprehend the ability *and limitations* of the vibrational qualities of essential oils to:

— affect the morphogenic fields of living systems,

— determine the structure of DNA/RNA, and

— alter the *structure and expression of dis-ease.*

It is important to understand then that *dis-ease is structured by consciousness into the subtle-energy body*, and that vibrational qualities (morphogenic fields) of vibrational tools such as essential oils have the ability to influence and *counter* (however temporarily) the morphogenic fields of dis-ease laid down by the structured consciousness of the fragmented Self.

When the proper oil is properly applied at the right time, essential oils can even stimulate our fragmented Self to permanently stop structuring dis-ease into our energy fields. That is, the oil can stimulate a release of consciousness from its trapped, fragmented structure into freely-radiating wholeness and allow for permanent healing of the body/mind, thus promoting true wholistic wellness through such a Self-realization.

Just why and how *consciousness* structures our subtle-energy fields and creates dis-ease can be understood by recognizing that human consciousness, sentience (self-awareness), or "Self" (Jung) has a fundamental need and drive for *unity*. This is not a new concept. Many ancient traditions, and even Freud himself, acknowledged this fundamental need in the human psyche for unity. Freud based *psychoanalysis* on the principle that the psyche could not hold two opposing elements simultaneously in awareness without creating the necessary tension to force a movement in the psyche to resolve the conflict toward a higher unity.

The tendency of the Self under stress and trauma is to fragment, and thereby *structure* its energy and awareness by splitting off pieces of self-aware being, hiding them from awareness in the unconscious. So the drive toward unity is blocked on this fundamental level of *the Self.* Psychologists call these splinters of Self "schizoid phenomena" and know that "schizoid splitting" occurs in all of us—especially early in life when we are vulnerable and helpless, or whenever profound trauma occurs. Psychologists also recognize the significant effects of *the splintered Self* in causing mental and physical illness.

One form of depth psychology that developed from Freud's thought, called *psychoanalysis*, focuses its theory on the schizoid mind (Fairbairn, Winnicott) and aims to unify the fragmented psyche (self). *How* psychoanalysis (or most of psychotherapy in general) usually attempts this is by a process of bringing into awareness *elements of mind* (thoughts, feelings, imagery, etc.) that are *symptoms* of the schizoid fragmenting of Self, <u>not</u> the fragments themselves. The hope is that this "*perturbing* of the unconscious" will reconnect the conscious mind with repressed elements (thoughts, feelings, etc.) and force a resolution as consciousness goes about its unifying ways. Remember, consciousness *loves* unity. Unity reflects our true nature as a seed of Oneness.

Psychoanalysis' reductionistic focus (a carry-over from the old paradigm of objective science and medicine) on *symptoms* of the body-mind, rather than *fragments of consciousness*, limits understanding and restricts the desired effect. This display of *bad faith* shows an inability to be in the *unknown*. But psychoanalysts would never admit to this, instead boasting of the need to be "responsible" and stay with the *known* they claim. Like the man who lost his keys mid-block at midnight, but instead searches under the lamppost on the corner because that's where he can "see", psychoanalysis —and most of psychology with it—has artificially and arbitrarily limited it's ability to perceive the true nature of the unconscious and to act on the fragmented Self (or its vibrational subplane) directly. Thus they cannot fathom or facilitate true whole being, much less *be* it themselves!

Likewise, some religious have reduced their vision to the *dogma* of a "God" *outside* them, as something disconnected from the Self, a 'projection.' Such a projected dogma (false knowing) prevents true knowledge, growth, and expansion into the wholeness ("holiness") of a united Self. This self-denial permeates and limits the entire expression of their life, sometimes including their view and use of vibrational tools like essential oils.

Enlightened (Postmodern) Approaches to Wellness

Thus, because of its *modern scientific and medical* origins in palliative (symptom-focused) medicine, psychoanalysis (Freud was a medical doctor) and the dynamic psychotherapies that arose from its influence are fundamentally different from an *enlightened postmodern process*. An enlightened approach to wholeness is necessarily *consciousness-based in its method* and does not focus on bringing elements of mind (thoughts, emotions, imagery) into awareness or on changing mental *symptoms*.

Instead, an enlightened approach focuses on *unifying consciousness* in a process that finds trapped fragments of conscious being as they are expressed in a person's life issues – then communicates directly with these self-aware, but unconscious parts of the Self toward their direct, conscious release into the awareness freely radiating in the body/mind. As a result of this un-structuring of fragmented consciousness (and its energy) into oneness, a shift in the structure and symptoms of dis-ease can occur resulting in true "holistic" health and well-being.

Such a self-unifying approach also differs with most *religious* intention in terms of where the religious devalue and detach from the physical to seek transcendence or later reward, which serves to *mystify* and un-ground (makes impersonal) one's sense of Self and reality. Psychiatrist Carl Jung, the founder of *analytical psychology,* noted the tendency of the religious to *project* what he called the "Self"–the potential of our conscious Being in its wholeness–*out there* as "God," thus separating it as an *idea*, and creating *a point of departure* from oneself and one's pain. This splitting and repression of awareness creates *a division within* the Self that then calls forth *dis-ease* (which Jung called the "neurotic synthesis") in order to gain attention and ultimately reunify its fragmented self.

In spite of this profound insight, Jung himself believed that the *unity* of conscious being, what he called the "Self," could *never* be attained. Psychoanalyst Wilfred Bion felt very much the same way about the wholeness he called "Truth" or 'O'. Instead, Jung felt that an individual endlessly moves toward unity of consciousness in a process he called "individuation," where one constantly swims in a soup of unconscious "archetypes" that surface in the psyche to influence consciousness as needed to move it toward balance and growth.

It was Jung's incomplete synthesis of pre-modern religious and modern scientific views that left him straddling the fence between the

two paradigms of science and religion and prevented him from seeing truly enlightened possibilities—the potential to fully unify the Self on its fundamental level by applying a postmodern view and method of unifying consciousness—a method that operates beyond a mere perturbing analysis of archetypal symptoms.

Enlightened *self-unifying methods* seek to ground consciousness (what religion more vaguely calls "spirit" or "soul") into the body/mind by finding and releasing the lost parts of one's conscious being. This is a very *personal and specific* process. In this, the enlightened paradigm is very much about grounding one *in* the world and their body-mind—rather than escaping it or alienating one from being fully in it—as with the ungrounded mysticism of religion or the alienating coldness (the "flatlander" view, as Einstein called it) of modern science. Instead, from a grounding of Self into the body-mind, the enlightened paradigm frees the individual to meaningfully *be*, *know,* and *do* their true Will, rather than that of another person's or group's *idea* of "God" or what otherwise is *thought* they ought to do or be. It is clearly about seeing oneself and life from well beyond the clinical, impersonal, materially-defined limits of modern science and medicine that (by a material default) confine one's view of life to the lie of a cold, meaningless, material-based existence with nothingness at both ends (before birth and after death).

While it's true that the limits of the religious and scientific paradigms are inherent in their particular world-view, ultimately the limits of their expression do not lie with them but in us. As with all tools, their use, good or bad, is in the hands of the holder. Science and religion are expressions of the collective consciousness. If the individual consciousness of those who form the collective is fragmented, the resulting cultural expression—scientific or religious—will surely reflect that fragmented being. But if the individual consciousness is whole, then truth, wholeness (holiness) and well-being are reflected. While there are those who have operated within these two previous world-views from wholeness, still these two paradigms inherently reflect the split in consciousness from which they arose. By their failure and limitation they beg to be transcended and enlightened by the postmodern paradigm.

The relevant question one might ask, as T.S. Elliot did in *The Love Song of J. Alfred Prufrock*, is "do I dare to perturb the universe," including the universe within? ***Due to their potent vibrational character and life-force, essential oils are wonderful tools for gently but powerfully perturbing the undiscovered Self to surface, release, and integrate—thus supporting a "metanoia," or paradigm shift toward unified being. This shift in the Self toward wholeness of conscious being brings with it a shift in thought and conceptualization. Primarily, thinking follows being, fragmented or whole.*** This is something those who seek to significantly change their being by changing their thoughts or words (using affirmations) ought to carefully consider.

Cognition at it base is an effect of consciousness, which is to say that thought is "sourced" by consciousness. When one is whole, this becomes obvious. When one is fragmented, the unconscious fragmented self takes over and shapes the thoughts to "think the thinker." Acting through the limbic system (the seat of emotion in the brain), events in consciousness affect the neuro-endocrine, neuro-muscular, and immune systems, "transcribing" (imprinting through the transcriptase enzyme) onto RNA (and from that onto DNA) the cellular biochemistry of dis-ease.

Coming from the other end of consciousness' effects on cell memory, the subtle vibration of fragmented consciousness similarly acts directly on DNA nucleic-acid patterning and structure (as noted in *Chapter 2*), and from its effects on DNA, templates dis-ease onto the RNA and cell organelles. So the body follows suit with the mind, being imprinted and structured by dis-ease.

Under the direction of consciousness, thoughts can act in the brain and body like opiates to kill pain, and are often used to medicate one's fears and repress trauma, repressing and anchoring emotion and trauma into the body. In this, their purpose is to hold one in place and avoid change, instituting the illusion of control. Both religious and scientific thought have been used for the purpose of controlling self and other. When used in a process of reuniting with repressed self-awareness, for example through the process of SelfQuesting , essential oils are a potent aid in piercing the veil, the cloud of (un)knowing structured in the physical, mental, and subtle bodies, and to bring us to something beyond mere intellectual thought. Thus, Truth comes to be found through an experience of Beauty, in OneSelf.

So the kind of knowing that comes from wholeness of Self is a knowing sourced *congruently* on all levels of our being (body, mind, energy, and awareness). When combined with a self-unifying process such as *SelfQuesting*, the vibrational and complex chemical nature of essential oils have a powerful ability to integrate all four levels of our being quickly and smoothly into a congruent wholeness. For this reason essential oils are frequently used at the end of a *SelfQuesting* session to aid *integration* of the new wholeness of consciousness into the lower levels of energy, mind, and body, as well as the outer life.

Consciousness, Essential Oils, and Our Outer World

So because the vibrational fields, created in Nature and preserved in the oils of plants, hold an energetic imprint of the Creator Consciousness, oils can influence the *structure of dis-ease* that the splintered Self has placed upon the subtle-energy fields of an individual's system. ***It is through this vibrational influence on the system's deep morphogenic ("form shaping") energy infrastructure that essential oils can stimulate one's conscious being (Self) toward wholeness and permanently reverse a dis-ease process.***

As one's consciousness becomes whole, this new wholeness un-structures the old energetic infrastructure of dis-ease toward holistic wellness and holiness. Because the Self is reflected in the outer world ("as above, so below"), this shift in consciousness can also change the *outer* environment of the individual to express this new wholeness—thus reflecting psychiatrist Carl Jung's concept of "synchronicity," the seeming non-causal "co-incidence" that reflects a deep connection between the psyche and the material world.

The optimal time to apply an essential oil (or any vibrational tool) is when the Self is ready to accept changes to its fragmented, structured consciousness (i.e. - has just released a fragment into oneness with the conscious self). Applying essentials oils 'by the book' is less likely to succeed in creating a powerful or permanent un-structuring of dis-ease if the system, the self, isn't ready to accept it. The fragmented self's *readiness* for a particular oil's vibrational influence on a needed shift can often be most accurately assessed by more flexible methods such as kinesiology, dowsing, or even more direct *intuitive* approaches. This optimizes one's ready acceptance of an essential oil's intervention.

Removing or neutralizing the underlying energetic infrastructure of dis-ease does not *guarantee* a healing of the body/mind, unless the necessary supports *on all levels* of one's being are present. A simple example of this would be if one denied themselves oxygen after releasing a part of Self into wholeness. No oxygen, no life, no healing—all four levels of reality require acknowledgement. However, supports to one's healing, oddly enough, begin to "show up" (co-incidently, synchronistically) in a person's life after sufficient wholeness of Self has been achieved. Suddenly, medical interventions, healing methods and other supports that weren't present before (or didn't work if they were) begin to appear or *now* work. [*Note*: See Chapter 5 for a list of supports, including essential oils, which have been found to be useful for integrating wholeness and supporting well-being in the body-mind.] Vibrational tools such as essential oils are very powerful in aiding the integration of wholeness into the body-mind and life, because of the potent life-force placed in them by Nature.

Enlightening Metaphors

To better understand the nature of consciousness and its power to influence energy fields, we can use 'light' as a *metaphor.* Translucent, full-spectrum, or "white" light has no color to the human eye; yet white light holds *all* colors. This can be seen when sunlight is sent through a leaded-glass prism and *fragments* into the various colors of the rainbow. Like white light, human consciousness in its wholeness *holds all structure and no structure*, which is to say that our conscious being (Self) was meant to shine freely, like the Sun—a point source radiating in all directions. Thus light is an excellent *metaphor* for consciousness.

White and yellow (gold) light traditionally have been used as symbols of oneness of consciousness, wholeness (holiness), as have the circle, sphere, and the Sun. These objects historically have held this meaning of unity in religious symbol, as is seen in the use of *radiant white or yellow-gold light,* the *Sun,* the circle or the *halo* in religious art.

Just as leaded glass is able to separate whole, white light from the Sun into fragments of varying color, so the "lead" (gravity, heaviness) of the fear-based and controlling ego fragments the unified, radiant consciousness of the Self into the darkness of the unconscious. This is *the alchemist's metaphor* that aims to "transmute" the *lead* of the fragmented self (the fear-based ego) into the *gold* of the unified Self (the *Philosopher's Stone*—the *Holy Grail* that *contains, grounds, and thus unifies conscious being* into oneness). In this transformation, lost fragments of the Self are brought into a unity of self-awareness, to freely radiate (like a star or the Sun [Son]) in oneness in the body/mind. Another metaphor for fragmented Self is seen when the tremendous gravity of a sun pulls itself (even its light) into "black holes" in a dark inner universe, which also happens to our consciousness when it fragments in times of trauma, and the 'gravity' of life (fear and pain) becomes too great.

From these similarities, recurring patterns in the seemingly random chaos of Nature, we begin to grasp the nature of consciousness and its connection to all of human existence—our body, mind, "spirit" and environment. Essential oils also reflect and are governed by this patterning within Nature, and share a special energetic healing relationship with us, since we exist together in Nature and arise from the same Superconscious Source.

Learning about the energy-shaping *patterns of frequency* that essential oils share with living systems, allows us to understand how these vibrational qualities of oils can be used to affect the energy fields of living creatures. But other recognizable patterns, by which Nature and human nature reveal themselves, also exist in our *language*.

Our Language Speaks to Us

Historical evidence for the existence, interplay, and influence of subtle "butterfly" levels of energy and consciousness, as well as the importance of wholeness, can be seen in the English language when we examine words like 'heal,' 'health,' 'holistic,' and 'wellness' or 'holy,' 'halo,' 'hallowed,' and 'holiness' or even the word 'wealth.' All these words have a *common origin* that reveals something important about us as individuals and about the true nature of the world.

Many English dictionaries note that these modern scientific or religious terms originate from the common root word, 'whole,' implying a need *to be whole*. This link in our language between health, the sacred, wealth, and wholeness speaks to a need to unite our fragmented, self-aware being into a oneness of consciousness—to unite on the deepest level of our being, that of our individual sentient Self. It also speaks to the profound results of uniting the Self: those of health, wealth, and holiness—all encouraged by the *un-structuring* of the consciousness of the splintered Self and a *restructuring* of the subtle energy fields affecting our body-mind, away from dis-ease toward wholeness (wellness). ***This is how essential oils can create well-being—by powerfully supporting consciousness toward wholeness and offering an alternate patterning of vibration. Essential oils alter the deep vibrational infrastructure of our being.***

The obviously common, but now lost meaning of *wholeness* shared by religion and science in words like 'health' and 'holiness,' points to an error in our present thinking that not only fails to link the two world-views of science and religion together meaningfully into a greater whole, but also fails to provide the *insight* needed to move toward un-structuring and unifying the splintered Self. This dilemma leaves our energy, mind, body, and our fragmented consciousness *structured for dis-ease.*

Reading the literature on essential oils, we often find a mixed use of old *scientific* and *religious* terms in naming and speaking of oils, oil blends, and their uses. Because the oils obviously work on most of the aspects of us that are described by religion or science, many find it necessary to use the varying languages of these often-conflicting world-views to try to fully describe essential oils and their various effects (physical, mental, energetic, spiritual).

But it's not necessary to limit or further fragment oneself with the divisive jargon and perspectives of these past world-views. By applying an expanded, enlightened world-view that recognizes and unifies *all* levels of human consciousness and understands their interrelations, we can *redefine* science and religion, and reconstruct language in terms of an *expanded* view of human consciousness and the Self, and thus move to unify and expand our expressions of ourselves. Then a *demystified and grounded* vision and way of speaking develops that is able to comprehend and express our full, true nature.

This grounded but expanded thinking (and language) empowers our ability to apply essential oils effectively, partly because it respects *both reason and intuition*, and thus involves more of self in the healing process (more whole-brained and fully-conscious). For example, if one stays with the "known" and reasons to apply essential oils "by the book," one quickly becomes confused by the various conflicting sources for understanding and applying oils and their limitations. If, however, one turns also to the more *intuitive* approaches to diagnosing and applying oils (such as kinesiology, dowsing, or even more refined and direct intuitive means, as with *SelfQuesting*), then a deeper understanding of the problem can be had, and a uniquely effective application of an essential oil can be more accurately undertaken—one specific to the person and problem being addressed *at that moment.*

Just as each individual is unique and each fragment of Self is uniquely structured and uniquely infrastructures dis-ease into the energy fields of the body-mind and life, so too must the application of essential oils be flexible and specific in supporting the needs of unraveling our uniquely-structured consciousness and energy.

Criticism of *intuitive* approaches by the scientific and medical community center around the idea that intuitive approaches "don't allow enough for scientific measurement and control," thus implying that a more measured and controlled means can be had—*one relevant to healing*. Such thinking avoids the fact that a *modern scientific* approach does not (and cannot, by definition) consider either the subtler *nonlinear dynamics* of human consciousness (the Self) or its energy, or unique biochemical energies, or how the unique dynamics of subtle energy, consciousness, and the healer-client relationship play into a healing process. All of this needs to be accounted for if healing is to be permanent and complete, affecting levels deeper than mere *symptoms* of mind/body dis-ease.

The source of all dis-ease is found in the Self. And it is in the Self and with vibrational tools like essential oils that dis-ease can strongly be shifted by poignant acts of profound Beauty. To limit one's focus to a `therapy' acting on a `disease' process misses the more expanded view of the person and their world required to create the vibrational change in the Self that reduces and eliminates the dis-ease. Because of inherent limits, science and religion *even together* do not address the needed expanded world-view and action on the Self. The postmodern, enlightened paradigm potentiates conscious *being,* and *action,* through acts of Beauty—and the Beauty of the Self—using tools from the bounty of Nature's life-force that exists within us and beyond us in essential oils.

"Sometimes it is easier to see more clearly into a liar than into the man who tells the truth. Truth, like light, blinds. Falsehood, on the contrary, is a beautiful twilight, that enhances every object."

— Albert Camus—

Revisiting Old Views

Most of modern science and religion are incapable of operating beyond a *twilight vision* that seeks to have their objects enhanced and clearly defined. This need for control paradoxically separates consciousness and the Self from the material, limiting one's options! Like an eye wincing in the blinding light of truth, unable to tolerate the *unknown potential* and personal experience that exists beyond the twilight of their perceived objects, science and religion blink and settle for an *idea* of reality. But large ideas block the full light of the Sun (Self) and cast large shadows in our unconscious that require attention to resolve.

Ideas have an intoxicating, sedating, opiate-like effect. And eventually the thoughts of science and religion come "to think the thinker" (Randall Eaton, *The Orca Project: A Meeting of Nations*) and alienate awareness. ***Modern science focuses on the material and in so doing objectifies human consciousness, while religion attaches itself to `spirit' (consciousness) as separate and transcendent of the material. Therein lies their fundamental difference, and their similarity, as both separate consciousness from the physical world. Any attempt to rectify this limitation by uniting religion and science also fails. It fails because individual human consciousness was meant to be whole and grounded fully in the body and in the world.*** As Carl Jung put it, "there can be no *spirit* without *instinct,* nor *instinct* without *spirit.*" Yet even here the sense of *two separate things* is apparent, and neither religion nor science, nor Jung's analytic psychology, can fully bridge the gap—the gap that the postmodern enlightened paradigm traverses toward OneSelf.

"All great truths begin as blasphemies."

—George Bernard Shaw—

This assessment of science and religion is not meant to negate the gains made by them, but to show their limits. Today's science and religion each are incomplete—being merely tools in the hands, mind, and awareness of the user—having been shaped by the minds of humans, according to their ability, and their level of development and wholeness. The author proposes a third, expanded and enlightened view in order to acknowledge aspects of reality that are important to understanding one's Self and its unity as a prime source of well being. Understanding how essential oils and other vibrational tools can assist to liberate the Self and empower it in ways not before experienced is part of that enlightened view.

The recently-accelerated rise in importance of themes of *unity* in science and religion (as well as in other human endeavors) signals our readiness to move beyond fear-based self-concepts, and beyond the separation and fragmentation within which science and religion organize incomplete images and reflections of ourselves and the world. What has become increasingly apparent is how these outdated self-images confine us individually and socially.

Nor are the assessments made here offered as *beliefs*; instead they are given for *consideration.* They are offered as an *expanded alternative* to the two previous world-views—an option heralding each individual's Self, in its *wholeness*, as the ultimate source for actualization, knowing. This option suggests a practical process by which true wholeness can be achieved, and thus by which individual consciousness and the physical can unite in a free, radiant, grounded, meaningful way—to exist and "be" beyond the thoughts that have *thought us* in the past. The reader is encouraged to throw off past self-concepts, to step into the unknown, and to *experience* and then decide for *themselves* the value of what is being related—in the absence of past infantilizing ideas or intimidating influences that have so limited our potential and self-expression, individual and cultural.

"Man's capacities have never been measured; nor are we to judge of what he can do by any precedents, so little has been tried."

—Henry David Thoreau—

"Those who have railed at metaphysics as an occult science will be as ashamed as those who railed at chemistry on the ground that pursuit of the Philosopher's Stone was illusory.... In the matter of principles there are only.... the experimental, everywhere and always. Greetings then to the new science which will change the orientation of human thought."

—Paramahansa Yogananda
(quoting Nobel Laureate in Medicine, Charles Richet, MD)—

4

Self-Questing™: enlightening consciousness with essential oils

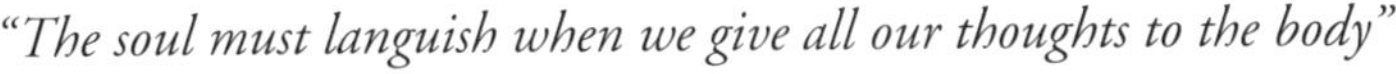

"The soul must languish when we give all our thoughts to the body"

— Mahatma Gandhi—

"So, you have inexplicably failed to isolate the Supreme Power in your test tubes?....examine your thoughts unremittingly for twenty-four hours. Then wonder no longer at God's absence."

—Sri Yukteswar, Yogananda's beloved teacher (to a noted chemist who doubted the existence of God because science hadn't detected Him.)—

Creating Whole States of Consciousness with Essential Oils

In noting the ability of essential oils to affect powerful levels of subtle energy and consciousness, we begin to demystify and better understand how essential oils can create great changes in our self-awareness, energy, mind, body, and life. One method of creating well-being that uses essential oils and gives great recognition to subtle energy and consciousness through a process of finding, releasing, and integrating fragments of one's conscious being, is *the SelfQuesting Approach*™. Unlike psychotherapy, which focuses its process on the *mind* and its feelings, thoughts, memories, and imagery, and unlike modern medicine that focuses on the body and its physical symptoms, *the SelfQuesting Approach*™ focuses its process on *individual consciousness* and its fundamental need to be unified, whole, and unstructured (freely radiating). *SelfQuesting*™ uses essential oils and other vibrational methods to assist finding, releasing, and integrating the energy and awareness of lost (unconscious) parts of the Self into the self-awareness radiating freely in the body/mind. *After* the Self has become relatively whole, *then* (if needed) medicine, psychotherapy, support tools (see below), etc. can better effect the changes for which they are intended, but might have been previously blocked from accomplishing.

Simply because *SelfQuesting*™ affects the feeling states, memories, imagery, and thought of an individual *does not* make it *psychotherapy*—any more than the fact that *SelfQuesting*™ and psychotherapy affect the body and disease means they are the practice of *medicine*. Medicine focuses mainly on physical effects on the *body*, while psychotherapy focuses on affecting and processing elements of *mind* (feelings, thoughts, memories, imagery). ***The SelfQuesting Approach™ focuses its process on finding and uniting consciousness, and arises from an expanded, enlightened, postmodern view of reality, not a modern scientific one, as psychotherapy, psychiatry, and medicine do.***

The SelfQuesting Approach™ effects its change on the Self and on the body/mind/energy system by connecting present-day issues—such as negative emotion (fear, anxiety, depression, loneliness, phobia, etc.), unwanted behavior (addiction, dependency, lack of motivation, confusion, paralysis, etc.), lack of meaning, relationship problems, lack of fulfillment, or physical issues—to fragments of Self trapped in the unconscious. After tracking and finding the trapped awareness by exploring the individual's presenting problems, *SelfQuesting*™ engages the fragment in an educational process of curiosity, to become aware of the who, what, where, when, and why of the separated awareness and update it with the conscious Self. The purpose of communicating and sharing awareness between the conscious self and the unconscious fragment is to quickly arrive at a rapprochement and *release* of the trapped awareness and its energy—an *un-structuring* and liberating of the fragmented consciousness into oneness. This release usually occurs in the same session that the fragment was discovered.

Operating in this direct manner on consciousness—by encountering real and potent parts of the Self, grounding their awareness in a process of Self-discovery in the unknown, and thereby freeing one's trapped awareness from delusion and false senses of certainty—is by definition and practice outside modern science, medicine, psychology, and religion. Since such a consciousness-based approach lies beyond the self-imposed limits of the two previous world-views of religion and modern science, no mere integration or *synthesis* of the two is sufficient to fully understand and describe the realities of such a process, or to create the "authentic excellence" (Eileen Watkins-Seymour & Clive Digby-Jones) facilitated by integrating all parts of the Self. Growing out of the postmodern enlightened paradigm, *the SelfQuesting Approach*™ is a different way of knowing and being, and a more profound means of uniting the Self, facilitating wholeness, and creating total well-being, than psychotherapy or medicine.

What generally is discovered in the *SelfQuesting*™ process is that what had been perceived as a significant trauma by the psyche caused part(s) of the Self, one's awareness and its energy, to split off from the conscious Self and structure within negative perceptions and emotions. This usually manifests as fear, but can elaborate into other feelings.

Once set in motion this "splinter Self" unconsciously goes about its task of acting on *fear-based goals* established at the time of fragmentation. This continues until such time that one becomes sufficiently aware of the fragment to be able to release it from unconsciousness into oneness with the conscious Self—to again freely radiate its lost energy and awareness in the body/mind.

Until this reunion with Self occurs, the fear-based, trapped awareness of the fragmented Self structures dis-ease into the energy, mind, body, and life of the individual, contributing further to the insecurity of a fractured ego already fearful of change and desiring control. The inherently insecure nature of the splintered Self often settles for a false sense of control and illusion in order to ease and avoid deep feelings of hopelessness, fear, and anxiety.

Postmodern Psycho-Religious Views of Wholeness and Fear

An illusory sense promising control and knowledge is often offered by the supposed *certainties* of science and religion, and supported by intimidation from their authorities, however subtle. Typically this authority is not based on *expertise* founded in experience, nor does it usually desire to lend a true learning experience, especially of oneself, instead prefering to be believed, obeyed, and followed unquestioningly.

The deep fear expressed in this desire for certainty and control is what British psychiatrist R.D. Laing called "ontological insecurity." An insecurity centered around a profound *fear of being*, particularly one's own being (Self) and its potential for freedom, expression, and fulfillment. An insecurity structured with the splintered Self.

> *"Our deepest fear is not that we are inadequate. Our deepest fear is that we are powerful beyond measure. It is our light, not our darkness that frightens us most... Your playing small does not serve the world. There is nothing enlightened about shrinking so that others won't feel insecure around you. We were born to manifest the Glory of God that is within each of us – not just in some of us, in everyone. And as we let our light*

shine, we unconsciously give others permission to do the same. As we are liberated from our fear, our presence automatically liberates others."

—Nelson Mandella (1994, Inaugural Speech,
quoting A Return to Love by Marianne Williamson)—

Over half a century ago psychoanalyst Eric Fromm explained in depth in his books *Escape From Freedom* and *The Art of Loving,* the psyche and behavior of one whose life is based on this insecurity of being. About that same time theologian Paul Tillich attempted to illuminate religious dogma on this issue in *The Courage to Be* and *The Dynamics of Faith,* which focused on grounding true religious experience and life by reframing religious themes to confront issues of insecurity and fear (of being). These writings appear to have remained inaccessible to many, not because the writings are *intellectually* difficult, but because another choice is often being made in terms of the purpose of our anxiety-driven use of religion, technology, science, and government. This choice aims to bury fear and insecurity, promote a false sense of knowing and control, and remain unconscious.

Jungian analyst Charles Hanna noted (in *The Face of the Deep*, 1967) that Tillich urged us to follow the Christian mystic Meister Eckhardt's vision and experience of God as "the Ground of our Being" (p. 144) and to move beyond the controlling ego's insecurity. Jung's own book *Psychological Types* (1923) affirmed Eckhardt's vision of God as the potential of our own conscious being (Self):

> "Hence for such a one "God has not yet become the world," says Eckhardt, since for him the world has taken the place of God [the Self]. Such a man has not succeeded in detaching and introverting the surplus value from the object ['God', lost Self], thus converting it

into [realizing it as] an *inner possession.* Were he *to possess it in himself* [reunite the Self] he would have God (this same value) continually as object or world, whereby God would become the world [one's world would be whole, reflecting OneSelf]. In the same portion Eckhardt says: "Whosoever is right in his feeling [OneSelf] findeth things fitting in all places and with all people, whereas he that is wrong findeth nothing right wherever or with whomever he may be. For a man of right feeling hath God within him [Self in wholeness]." A man who has this value in himself [OneSelf] is everywhere well-disposed: he is not dependent upon objects, i.e., he is not forever needing and hoping from the object [the world] what he himself lacks [wholeness]."

—C. G. Jung, *Psychological Types*, 1923, p.306
(Italics and words in [...] are mine)—

With this in mind, we can cut to the chase to move beyond earth-bound scientific or spirit-bound religious dogmas that separate us and our consciousness from being fully in the body, that are based in this *universal* insecurity of being, and that fail to challenge and truly *transform* the fear-based ego. We can arrive at a postmodern understanding of the need to unify the fragmented Self, thereby eliminating the true *cause* of the *ontological insecurity* that drives us to choose these self-limiting ways of knowing and being. We can choose to break the cycle of modern limitation by the *act* of bringing the Self into wholeness, becoming OneSelf. And we can then reshape our thinking in the light of this new being and wholeness, and precipitate further challenge and growth.

Questing Wholeness with Essential Oils

SelfQuesting, as its name implies, is such a quest for the Self—to find one's fragmented lost consciousness, and release and integrate that trapped energy and awareness back into radiant wholeness in the body/mind. *SelfQuesting* is a direct method to identify, contact, communicate, and release these trapped parts of Self. This focus is the source of SelfQuesting's power and differentiates it from other forms of healing, such as modern medicine, psychotherapy, vibrational medicine, prayer, etc., which generally don't sufficiently provide the necessary enlightened appreciation of consciousness, within a process of communication, for the needed awareness and connection with Self to occur.

Essential oils are an important aid in helping the body-mind-energy system to integrate the wholeness of Self that is created by the *SelfQuesting* process. Without the aid of essential oils and other vibrational methods, this *integration* and *un-structuring* of imbalances (caused by fragmentation) can create considerable mental, emotional, and behavioral disturbance, as well as physical discomfort, as wholeness integrates into a body/mind what has long been configured according to fragmentation.

With the introduction of essential oils and other vibrational aids to the Self-Questing process most of the unpleasantness associated with integration is eased and avoided. The result is that difficulties arising after a *SelfQuesting* session usually will have to do with the *next* fragment surfacing for attention, and can be dealt with as such in the next session, rather than being confused with the *integration* process from the last part released.

In addition, essential oils can assist during the *SelfQuesting* sessions directly in the release and unification of the separated consciousness, and thus serve as more than simply an integration tool. **Again, the profound positive effects, when applying the *optimal* essential oil *at the right time*, are due mainly to the vibrational qualities of essential oils and their ability to shift the individual's underlying energetic infrastructure (morphogenic field) of dis-ease, and so support an integration of the new wholeness into the body/mind as wellness.**

Care should be taken, however, when using a vibrational method or tool (such as an essential oil) to release a fragment. The application of potent vibrational methods *too soon*, before sufficient conscious processing has occurred to prepare the fragment for release, can create a pre-emptive, partial release of *symptoms,* not necessarily the consciousness itself. This results in a loss of contact with the part, as well as a countering disturbance or "dis-ease" in the body/mind, often experienced as confusion, but not limited to that. This will require re-engaging the process and fragment at that or another time (when accessible) in order to ease the disturbance created by such a premature and incomplete release.

A vibrational tool shouldn't be used as a shortcut to <u>force</u> the resolution of symptoms or the release of a fragment, because if there is a failure to release, negative side effects are likely. The disturbance to a person's system and life, caused by such a failed attempt, is usually not serious but can be uncomfortable, and provides an important lesson in regard to the limits of vibrational tools.

In short, there's no substitute for the *necessary increase in awareness* between the conscious Self and the fragment under investigation. (*Note*: This is not a matter of "right or wrong." Any process of questing Self is fraught with unknowns and incomplete actions right up to the point of full release and union. But in the session, the practitioner must be able to *stay in the unknown* with the client whose quest is being facilitated. He must wade through the "errors" and uncertainty with the client without foreclosing on the exploration by putting his own "stuff" into the process, and <u>without needing to force the issue in any way</u>. The use of intuitive methods, such as kinesiology, dowsing, or more direct intuitive methods, can help to keep the practitioner focused, and help to determine the necessity and optimal time for application of an essential oil or other vibrational tool. In this way, the *means* of the process is consistent with the *end.* The *process* then becomes unifying, whereby the client and facilitator quest together in the unknown to discover and release the client's fragmented consciousness into wholeness, and from that wholeness promote well-being on all levels).

Identifying the Need for Self-Questing

All issues and difficulties that one encounters in life—whether they manifest as physical, mental, behavioral, energetic, existential, spiritual, or within or outside oneself—are expressions of a splintered Self, a fragmented diminishing of one's consciousness. Thus, it could be generally said that *any* discomfort experienced in life is grounds for a quest to resolve the *fundamental cause,* and suggests the need for a process to unify the Self. Certainly those who wish to optimize their life and create meaning, wellness, joy, and abundance would find the wholeness brought on by a unifying process like *SelfQuesting* to be greatly satisfying, eventually leading to the certainty of why it was *necessary* to quest the Self in this particular way.

More specifically, however, there are experiences common to many of us that can be drawn upon to understand and relate to the need for *SelfQuesting.* For example, we all have experienced times when, no matter how strong our desire, or how much will power or determination we apply, we simply cannot force ourselves to accomplish a task or avoid a compulsion. The sense often is that "something else just takes over and *I lose focus* of who I am and what's important." That 'something' that 'takes over' is the unconscious fragmented Self. It can dictate our behavior, sensation, belief, thought, emotion, drive, or even the physical state of our body—healthy, tired, shaky, paralyzed, dis-eased, agitated, depressed, etc. (Recall the *physical* results of fragmented consciousness noted previously in the medical study of dissociation [multiple personality] in *Chapter 2*).

Many wonder why, no matter how much analysis or feeling has been experienced around an issue, the same life patterns and occurrences continue to repeat. One often finds oneself facing the same old issues arising in one's emotions, relationships, job, or in the body—in spite of how much *catharsis, insight, or healing* one might have experienced around the issue from psychotherapy or medicine. While the *symptoms* of the underlying problem might have been repeatedly addressed (and even relieved for a time), the fundamental *cause* of the symptoms or issues, the fragmented Self, has not been fully resolved into unity, and so the dis-ease remains anchored in the body-mind.

Disunity of consciousness (Self) creates dis-ease and difficulty for a purpose; it does so in order to get our attention and come back into unity. The fact that the fragmenting of our conscious being (Self) structures dis-ease into all levels of our system (identity, energy, mind, body) and in our outer life as well, is a fundamental law of human existence. It is one that must be addressed at that fundamental level, by uniting consciousness, if we wish to achieve well being.

Enlightened Choices

In the supposed certainty of their *way of knowing*, psychology, medicine, and religion often tell us that we need to resolve ourselves to accepting our condition (whatever it is) and suggest that it is largely fixed and unchangeable, or even "God's inscrutable decree." Once accepted, this kind of submissive view of reality dooms one to judge all else as 'fantasy,' limits choice, and dis-empowers. However, if we are of sufficient mind and heart to quest an expanded concept of reality and ourselves—one *grounded* in the realities recognized by religion and science, but whose grasp transcends and bridges these incomplete views by acknowledging Self-truths that they cannot—then we can open to, and empower, new and creative options drawn from infinite possibility.

The enlightened paradigm suggests such a resolution. It begins with our view of ourselves, and then points to the possibility of *a profound change of being and heart*—what the Greeks call "metanoia." What specifically is offered by the enlightened paradigm is a new *personal* vision, an expanded state of self-awareness, and *an approach* to resolving the fragmented Self into oneness. This is not accomplished in some *vague* manner or understood by some mysterious, mystical idea. Instead, by applying what is already known about the schizoid mind (the fragmented psyche) and how it affects our body/mind and life, a method is undertaken that is *consistent* with the end of creating a unified Self—it is a process grounded in a profound and real *understanding* of ourselves and the nature of our *conscious being*.

Essential oils, or other vibrational tools and methods, alone have in some cases been able to precipitate such a metanoia, a complete shift in one's being, that resolved significant life issues (mental, physical, behavioral, environmental, etc.), allowing for fulfillment and joy. But typically a more *conscious* approach—one directed at finding the trapped awareness holding the Self—is first needed to obtain the unified self-awareness necessary to allow for *total wellness*.

The potent role that essential oils as vibrational tools can play in the quest for a whole Self cannot be overstated. Because of their ability to affect the subtle energy fields that structure dis-ease into the body-mind, essential oils are often truly "essential" to this process, allowing for a smooth transition to wellness. In cases of great distress or resistance, essential oils have allowed for a session to take place, and for a session's subsequent effects on wellness to be accomplished, where none could have without its application.

5

Recommended vibrational tools and supports

"Chitragupta, who is supposedly writing our deeds in an account book, is no other than the conscious and unconscious mind. The Lord of Law, to whom we have to render the account, is the Soul [consciousness hidden] within us."

— Gopal Singh—

Acknowledging All Levels of Our Being

If we are to have wellness, meaning, and abundance in our life, *all* levels of our system require acknowledgement—body, mind, energy, and consciousness—as well as our outer life. This becomes more obvious as we, in our conscious being, become more whole and *grounded in the body/mind.* Thus, we are more *aware* of ourselves and more cognizant of the broad spectrum of life's realities.

The recommendations that follow focus on supporting the needs of the body, mind, energy, and conscious Self during transition to wholeness and thereafter. They are *suggestions* and by no means complete, but have shown to generally support the system and enhance the quest for wholeness and well-being. ***These support recommendations are not meant as a substitute for the necessary process of bringing one's conscious being (Self) into unity, though they'll serve to assist one in coming into that wholeness.*** The Self is the primary agent, in its wholeness or fragmentation, that structures well-being or dis-ease, even affecting one's abundance, outer life, and environment (synchronicity).

It's typical for the person undergoing a transformational process through the *SelfQuesting Approach*™ to witness a positive shift in the effectiveness and appearance of products and methods that assist their body/mind to achieve wellness. Often this includes a dramatic increase in the effectiveness of products and methods that had already been tried but which were not effective until a certain level of wholeness was achieved, and thus the Self *allowed* such a shift.

So, it's not uncommon to see medicines, remedies, herbs, foods, supplements, essential oils, or healing methods such as medicine, psychotherapy, energy healing or ritual (prayer, meditation, etc), that previously had little or none of their intended positive effect, to suddenly become effective with *SelfQuesting* sessions or, to suddenly appear and "resonate" with the client, assisting in their healing process at various levels. *SelfQuesting* also facilitates growth and acceptance of one's *intuitive faculties* and a willingness to follow them, further leading to the timely discovery of new and particularly effective products, methods, and behaviors that aid abundance and well being.

Tools and Supports For The Body-Mind Energy System

Outlined below are suggestions for proven supports. ***Do not underestimate the power of even one of them to move you toward well-being!*** Without taking from modern medicine its due credit, it's nonetheless important to note that the results of these supportive procedures alone will give you a new perspective on the *misdirection* of modern medicine, and the attention, expense, and politics that have been misplaced there. Still, again, allopathic interventions will become *more effective* with *SelfQuesting,* eventually becoming less needed.

After boosting the immune system and supporting the colon, nutritional assistance from whole-food supplements such as MSM (especially when empowered with wolfberry), plant greens like blue-green algae, and other whole, raw, vegan foods are recommended. Again, do not underestimate the power of these nutritional substances to support the body/mind! Essential oils play an important role as *physical* supports, and also as part of a program to support one emotionally and psychologically during times of transformation when subtle inputs ("butterflies") tend to have even greater impact.

In addition to essential oils, recommendations are given here for other vibrational tools. Major improvements to one's well-being can typically be experienced by following any one of these recommendations, but *combined* they constitute an exceptionally powerful program for *synergistically* supporting wellness. Readers are encouraged to proceed at their own pace, a speed that is comfortable and easy for them, without burdening or overloading themselves. It is also advised that common sense be used when employing these recommendations, and, when a medical condition is presenting, they probably should not be undertaken against or without the advice of a physician. (See below for recommendations on choosing a "holistic" physician.)

Beyond therapeutic-grade essential oils, one of the most *powerful* and important recommendations made below is a vibrational method that, like essential oils, is used as an important adjunct to assist the *SelfQuesting Approach*, called *the Power Tap*™. *The Power Tap*™ draws on the best aspects of Emotional Freedom Technique and Thought Field Therapy and is discussed further in the "energy supports" section below. Detailed instructions with a diagram can be obtained at *www.selfquesting.com*. This technique is very effective for clearing negative mind-body issues resulting from energy blocks created by fragmented consciousness.

A Brief Overview of Vibrational Tools:

Young Living Essential Oils® - the premier essential oils company of North America, and the only one that thoroughly tests all its oils for quality and purity using gas chromatography and mass spectroscopy. Young Living has a wide range of superb products (single oils, oil blends, food supplements cleaning products, personal and skin care, etc.) all of which put essential oils to work to great benefit. While essential oils have been around and proven for millennia, their use is still in its infancy as far as creating whole being and supporting total wellness. Young Living is on the leading edge of this quest. Quality-proven oils give their products a significant edge that cannot be matched elsewhere.

The Power Tap ™ - a quick and powerful technique to clear negative body-mind states (emotions, pains, issues, thoughts, addictions, behaviors, etc.). Distilled from years of research into energy-meridian tapping and eye-movement techniques, the Power Tap™ is easier to learn, simpler to apply, and more effective than other similar clearing techniques. (For a diagram with instructions see www.selfquesting.com.)

The Chi Machine® - a very powerful wellness device that oxygenates, detoxifies, and moves lymph like no other tool. While one lies on their back this machine moves the feet from side to side creating a figure 8 motion in the body that turns on "chi" and pumps body fluids (spinal, blood, lymph, etc.) to detoxify, nourish, and oxygenate. Developed by a former president of the Japanese Oxygen Association, the effects of this tool (while subtle to the user) produce profound results bringing about balance and well being. Use cautiously; build slowly (in terms of time used) to avoid detoxifying too quickly!

Bikram Yoga® - Developed under medical supervision in India by Bikram Choudhury—an award-winning, internationally-acclaimed Yogi—this style of yoga uses medically and scientifically proven yoga postures performed in a room at 110 degrees F. The results on the body-mind and consciousness of the practitioner are quite profound in terms of fitness, health, awareness, and well being. For those seeking a gentler approach to exercise and building wellness, Kali Ray Yoga offers an excellent program for building wellness at your own, stress-free speed. There are great DVDs that can be used at home.

Rawfood Diet – the diet we were put on this planet to eat! The only one we've adapted to and can be healthy on. Tired of being sick, fat, and tired? Put the excuses away and try it! Visit a rawfood restaurant (google it) to see how good it can be! A better way of living and being! Go slowly into raw; knowledge is everything.

Holosync® from Centerpointe® - Ever wonder why the East Indians have praised the benefits of meditation to the body, mind, and spirit for 5,000 years? Centerpointe has packaged special audio CD recordings to trigger these benefits for the time-crunched Westerner, providing whole-brain wellness benefits (from theta and delta brainwaves) of decades of disciplined meditation. Wow!...try it!

Related Links

www.youngliving.com/selfquest - SelfQuest's Young Living Oils® site
www.hteamericas.com - the Chi Machine® site
www.bikramyoga.com/ - the Bikram Yoga site
www.triyoga.com - Kali Ray Yoga site (great DVD's for at-home use!)
www.centerpointe.com - Centerpointe site for the Holosync CD's.
Rawfoods: see sunfood.com, JuiceFeasting.com, treeoflife.nu.

Contrary to what one might believe, wholeness is not a term describing some vague *mystery*. Rather, when applied to a person, wholeness describes a uniform un-fragmented state of fully conscious Self-awareness from which one's existence manifests according to one's wholeness of *conscious being* and its unified intent (Will). The psychiatrist Carl Jung called this unity of individual consciousness the "Self" (with a capital 'S' to reflect a *reverence*).

By definition, "wholeness" speaks to *all* of what it describes, not just some part of it. When describing an individual, wholeness speaks to that person being whole on *all levels of their existence – consciousness, energy, mind,* and *body*—as well as to their functioning and relating in life, and how their life manifests.

Four Levels/Orders of Reality *(ordered least-to-most causal)*

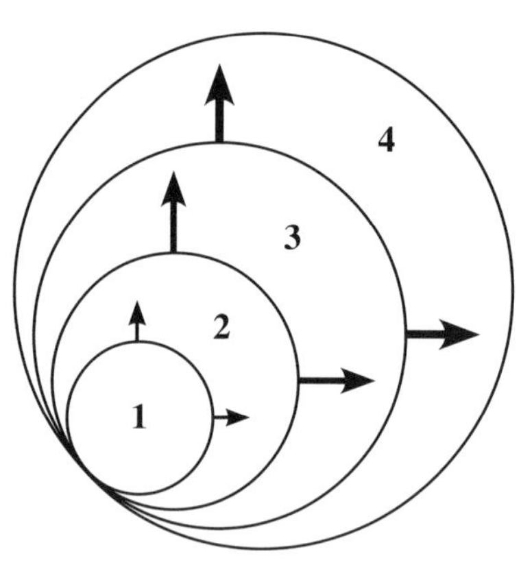

1. **MATTER/BODY** - the material world of objects & the body. (Medicine's focus).
2. **MIND** - thought, emotion, imagery - structures of mind. (Psychology's focus).
3. **ENERGY** - the generative 'implicate order' or 'quantum holomovement' in physics. Known to some as the 'Tao,' or "the Mother of the Ten Thousand Things." (Essential Oil's focus).
4. **CONSCIOUSNESS** - philosophy's Initial Cause or Truth. Ancient wisdom's Unity, the Ground of Our Being, Presence, Superconscious awareness. (SelfQuesting's focus).

To build *total* wellness *all levels of reality* must be acknowledged. It stands to reason that if tools are used that powerfully influence all *four* levels of reality—the *physical*, the *mental*, the *energetic*, and the deep causal level of *consciousness* (Self)—then wellness can most optimally and quickly be built. In an unusually powerful way, these tools provide the Self support on these various levels. They also assist the *integration* of wholeness of consciousness brought about by *SelfQuesting*™ into the body, mind, and life. But as stand-alone aids for wellness and for the promotion of whole being, the tools listed above and explained in detail below are very powerful. Together in *synergy* their effect is far "greater than the sum of their parts."

Consciousness is that subtle but powerful "butterfly" that causes tornadoes in the body, mind, energy, and life. When the butterfly of consciousness becomes "bottled" (trapped) in the unconscious, it creates tornadoes of dis-ease in our system and life. Likewise essential oils are also "butterflies in a bottle"—containing subtle energies that can be released for well being.

Vibrational Tools

The tools shared here are "vibrational" in that they serve to assist in moving one toward conscious, whole (well) being by affecting *subtle energy*. These tools act primarily through their positive effect on what Rupert Sheldrake called the "morphogenic" (form-shaping) fields of subtle, vibrational energy that we each consist of and our system is directed by. These morphogenic fields of subtle energy determine the structure and function of our body/mind, shaping wellness or dis-ease. Thus consciousness—*the prime director* structuring our energy and from that our mind, body, and life—is the *fundamental level* requiring attention if we are to create whole being. Yet acknowledgement of less causal levels of energy, mind, and body is also required.

So, while oneness of conscious being is a necessary condition for an individual to be whole, it might not be sufficient to create the expression of whole being on all levels. The vibrational tools offered here support this expression of wholeness into these lower levels, and work in synergy with SelfQuesting™.

A Commitment... and a Necessity

Creating wholeness is not difficult, but it requires discipline and persistence. Today we're exposed to more personal and environmental stresses in a week than our ancestors were exposed to in their entire life. These stresses and pollutants take a toll on our well being. Creating wellness today requires insight, discipline, and commitment, as well as time to take effect, and it must become *a way of living and being*. Nothing short of this will create well-being and happiness. To fail is to court dis-ease and fall short of one's birthright of fulfillment and joy. ***Well-being is a lifestyle directed by being whole, OneSelf.***

Unless one is willing to waste their potential for well-being and wholeness, one needs to take responsibility and *commit* to the knowledge, discipline, heart, and action required. If one applies *the SelfQuesting Approach*™ and the tools shared here, they can create a level of wellness, joy, and success rarely experienced. Evolving to live better than kings, the users of these tools can powerfully step up to their birthright—to live like the "gods" that perennial wisdom, scripture, and intuition have long and clearly told us we are. When properly applied, the benefits to one's health, success, and wholeness generated by these tools – especially through their *synergistic* use in combination – will be powerful, immediate, and grow stronger over time.

Young Living Essential Oils®

"And He shall know His children by their scent."

— Script found with essential oil relics linked to Christ—

The lifeblood of an aromatic plant is its essential oil, which holds its life-force. When properly grown, handled, processed and stored, the essential oils of these plants have a potent healing biochemistry and provide a vibrational medicine—a profoundly life-affirming influence that has just begun to be understood in its depth and wonder. Unfortunately, virtually all essential oils (and many herbs) sold today fail to live up to their promise because they are improperly grown, modified, diluted, mishandled, or otherwise fractionated or adulterated.

The only North American essential oil supplier (and one of the few in the world) that applies ISO AFNOR "Therapeutic-Grade" quality standards and uses *gas chromatography / mass spectrograph (GC/MS)* analysis to confirm the presence of the full spectrum of an oil's proper constituents and to eliminate the potential for adulterants, cutting agents, synthetic oils, etc., is *Young Living Essential Oils® (YLEO)*. Since the use of adulterants, diluting agents, etc. is rife in the industry, the only sure method of detecting adulterants is to perform *GC/MS* (many adulterants are clear, odorless, or otherwise undetectable). Unless *GC/MS* is performed, one cannot know what an essential oil consists of. Therefore an essential oil cannot truthfully be claimed to be "therapeutic grade" without this analysis. Essential oils have the uncanny ability to penetrate quickly and deeply into the body carrying coexisting chemicals with them. For this reason, in creating and supporting whole being, essential oils that have not been confirmed pure and proper by *GC/MS (or NMR)* are *substandard* for use in any kind of therapy.

Young Living® has created a terrific product line of truly therapeutic grade single oils and wondrous essential oil blends, and also integrated them into a host of toxin-free food supplements, personal and skin care products, home cleaning products, and other related wellness items that are state of the art and *very* trustworthy. The owner Gary Young will not sell what he won't use on himself and his family (who are very dear to him), and he is very strict about what he considers worthy of use. *YLEO* has now expanded into Europe, Australia, Japan, and South America. As of 2007 *YLEO* had over *one million acres* planted worldwide in the production of essential oils. Administratively, *YLEO* is very forward looking and poised for growth. And their customer service is top notch!

The wellness industry is set to become a *trillion* dollar industry by 2010, as aging baby-boomers turn more and more to their inevitable health and longevity needs. *Young Living,* with great vision and heart, has positioned itself better each year as a leader in the wellness industry. As people worldwide turn from *Big Pharma's* profit-driven control of modern medicine toward more workable alternative approaches to well-being, the efficacy of *YLEO's* truly "therapeutic grade" essential oils—placed synergistically into *YLEO* wellness products—will prove more and more to be well ahead of the competition. The *YLEO* compensation plan is among the best in the network marketing industry. In a world of shaky employment, a growing and sound home-based business can provide a much needed security. What's more, aiding others toward wellness provides life with a meaning and purpose beyond words or monetary value.

Young Living is a heart-filled company with no-nonsense products. You do yourself and your loved ones a disservice by not participating. True "therapeutic grade" essential oils are perhaps the most powerful vibrational tools on the planet. Alone, or used *synergistically* in combination with other proven tools like the *Chi Machine®*, *Holosync®*, *Bikram Yoga®*, *the Power Tap™*, and as an aid to *SelfQuesting™*, oils provide an *unmatched wellness tool* that is indispensable in today's quick-changing world of toxins, stress, death, and dis-ease for profit, and to our profound needs for fulfillment in life.

If you will allow yourself to step into a personal quest that integrates left-brained reason with right-brained intuitive experience, adding proper quality *essential oil use* as part of that journey, you will find a whole-brained and heartfelt flowering of Self will occur. When properly integrated with a method like *the SelfQuesting Approach™* you can arrive at a place that on the one hand is unlike anything you've ever experienced in terms of fulfillment and on the other hand deeply and personally familiar, like a "coming home."

Call the *SelfQuesting Center for Whole Being™* and become introduced to *Young Living Esssential Oil* products today (or see our *YLEO* website *www.youngliving.com/SelfQuest*). A good place to start experiencing *YL* oils is their *Essential 7 Kit* or the emotional and consciousness oil blends of the former *Feelings Kit* and *7th Heaven Kit,* which blends can still be bought individually (though at this time they are no longer available as *kits*)—see charts on next page. The YLEO *Thieves* product line of cleaning and personal care products is an outstanding, affective alternative to the abundance of toxic cleaners, soaps, toothpastes, mouthwashes, etc, currently on the market.

Feel free to call and consult with the *SelfQuesting Center™* regarding your specific needs. We offer workshops and seminars in the use of essential oils to facilitate whole states of consciousness, to heal damaged emotions and to clear cellular memory. Contact us for current events or to inquire about the possibility of arranging a workshop in your area on the intuitive use of essential oils to heal negative emotion and expand the Self (*www.selfquesting.com*).

The Principal Consciousness Oil Blends (YLEO)

SINGLE OIL INGREDIENTS

OIL BLEND	Angelica	Blue Tansy	Cedarwood	Chamomile *(Roman)*	Cinnamon Bark	Frankincense	Geranium	Helichrysum	Hyssop	Jasmine	Juniper	Lavender	Melissa	Myrrh	Neroli	Rose	Rosewood	Sandalwood	Spruce	Ylang Ylang	Citrus *(See below)*	ADDITIONAL INGREDIENTS
Abundance					■	■								■					■			Clove, Patchouli, Ginger
Acceptance		■				■	■								■		■	■				
Awaken *s*	■	■		■		■	■	■	■	■	■	■	■		■	■	■	■	■	■	*o,l,m,t,b*	
Christmas Spirit					■														■		*0*	
Citrus Fresh																					*o,l,t,m,g*	Spearmint
Dream Catcher *s*		■									■						■	■	■	■	*t,b*	Anise, Black Pepper
Forgiveness *f*	■			■		■	■	■		■		■	■			■	■	■			*l,b*	Palmarosa
Gathering *s*					■	■	■					■				■		■	■	■		Galbanum
Gentle Baby				■			■			■		■				■	■			■	*l,b*	Palmarosa
Grounding *f*	■		■								■								■	■		Sage, White Fir, Pine
Harmony *f*	■			■		■	■		■	■		■				■	■	■	■	■	*o,l,b*	Palmarosa
Hope *f*				■							■		■	■					■			
Humility *s*						■	■						■	■	■	■	■			■		Spikenard
Inner Child *f*										■					■			■	■	■	*o,t*	Lemongrass
Inspiration *s*			■			■											■	■	■			Myrtle, Mugwort
Into the Future			■			■				■	■									■		Clary Sage, Idaho Tansy, White Fir, White Lotus
Joy *f*				■			■			■						■				■	*l,m,b*	Palmarosa
Motivation				■								■							■	■		
Peace & Calming		■																		■	*o,t*	Patchouli
Present Time *f*															■				■	■		
Release *f*		■					■					■						■		■		
Sacred Mtn. *s*			■																■	■		Idaho Balsam Fir
SARA *f*		■	■				■					■				■				■	*o*	White Lotus
Sensation										■							■			■		
Trauma Life						■	■	■				■				■		■	■			Valerian, Davana, C. Hystrix
Valor *f*		■				■											■		■			
Wht. Angelica *f,s*							■		■				■	■		■	■	■	■	■	*b*	

f Part of original Feelings Kit
s Part of original Seventh Heaven Kit

b=bergamot *m=mandarin*
g=grapefruit *o=orange*
l=lemon *t=tangerine*

Suggested Application Areas for the Consciousness Oils (YLEO)

■ Main
▲ Optional

Also, oils can be applied to most *areas of concern* related to the work being done. The correct use of dowsing, kinesiology, etc. to aid intuitive decision-making is advised.

OIL BLEND	Brain Stem	Chest	Crown	Difuse	Ears	Face	Feet	Forehead	Heart	Horns *(above temples)*	Liver	Navel	Neck	Nose	Shoulders	Solar Plexus	Temples	Thymus	Wear as a perfume	Wrists	ADDITIONAL AREAS
Abundance				▲	■	▲							■						▲	■	Carry in wallet/purse
Acceptance		▲		▲		▲	▲		▲				▲							▲	Base of spine
Awaken *s*				■				■	▲										■	▲	Bath, massage
Christmas Spirit				▲																	
Citrus Fresh				▲	▲				▲											▲	Bath, massage
Dream Catcher *s*				■	▲			▲									▲		■		Throat, third eye
Forgiveness *f*					▲				▲			■							■	▲	Behind the ears
Gathering *s*		▲		■		▲		▲	▲			■					■	▲		▲	
Gentle Baby				▲		▲	▲														Massage, back and stomach
Grounding *f*	■			▲													▲				Back of neck, sternum
Harmony *f*				▲	▲		▲		▲										▲		Chakras, areas of poor circulation
Hope *f*				▲	■															▲	
Humility *s*				■					▲								▲		■		
Inner Child *f*				▲								■									
Inspiration *s*				■				▲		▲									■		Back of neck
Into the Future				▲					▲											▲	Bath, massage
Joy *f*				■				▲		■									■	▲	Bath, VitaFlex on heart point
Motivation		▲		▲	▲		▲					▲							▲		Big toes, neck nape, palms
Peace & Calming	▲			■		■	▲												▲		Back of neck, back, bath
Present Time *f*				▲				▲										■	■		Sternum
Release *f*					■		▲				■								▲		VitaFlex on liver points
Sacred Mtn. *s*	▲		▲	■															■	▲	Behind ears
SARA *f*		■		■			▲					■					▲				VitaFlex on feet
Sensation				▲															▲		Bath, massage
Trauma Life	■			▲			▲			▲		▲	▲	▲				▲		▲	VitaFlex on big toe
Valor *f*				▲	▲		■									▲		▲		▲	VitaFlex on feet
Wht. Angelica *f,s*				■										▲	■		▲		■		VitaFlex on feet

f Part of original Feelings Kit
s Part of original Seventh Heaven Kit

Essential oils greatly assist ones Yoga and rawfood practices. Your yoga instructor will likely not inform you of this, nor will your typical rawfoodist, as their experience with oils has been corrupted by their experience with oils in perfumes and other polluted sources that create weak or even negative results due to their toxic or missing constituents. Some individuals, due to their own toxic state, will react badly to even truly pure essential oils—as the essential oils mobilize toxins in their body and trigger a "cleansing reaction," or cause a mobilizing of unprocessed emotions and issues in their psyche, which even Yoga or a rawfoods diet might not yet have been able to mobilize.

My policy regarding others and my use of essential oils is as follows: I take responsibility for using only truly pure, "therapeutic grade" essential oils, which I *know* are pure because they have been tested by *gas chromatography (etc.)*. ***I do not take responsibility for the toxic reactions of others to my use of truly pure oils***. Nor do I take responsibility for what the uninformed (or those who choose not to be accountable for their own toxic state) might like to displace onto me or oils.

This having been said, as a rule I *prefer* not to offend others, create discomfort for them, or thwart their will. I do however reserve my *right* to do what I need to do for myself, especially when I know it is benign (and even helpful!) in regard to others. I therefore use essential oils in my yoga practice, but try to keep any *external* application to a minimum and/or allow the application of an oil to "age" on my body a half hour or more before I go out in public.

In one's Yoga practice, I strongly recommend using *Young Living Essential Oils*® both for their trusted *true* purity and their powerful balancing and wholing effects. An hour before the start of a yoga class, I ingest a

Longevity Capsule (a blend of orange, clove, frankincense and thyme in a gelatin capsule). Having been encapsulated in an enteric-coated gel cap, it is designed to be released into the intestine, bypassing stomach acidity. These essential oils:

- Regulate blood density
- Increase oxygen availability
- Bind heavy metals for release from the body
- Neutralize acidity and toxins mobilized by the Yoga (the heat and intensity of the postures)
- Repair DNA/RNA
- Regulate the body's heat and use of water
- Regulate the endocrine system and blood sugar
- Have many other benefits.

Properly used, essential oils will only move to naturally balance the system. Essential oils will never drive the body, mind, energy, or spirit to an extreme beyond its proper, natural balance.

I also place 2 drops each of lemon and peppermint oil in my drinking water (with *stevia* - a natural, non-caloric sweetener) for drinking before, during, and after the Yoga class, which further aids the body to balance, regulate heat and blood density, neutralize toxins and acidity, etc. In today's world of "better living through chemistry" we hold vast amounts and types of toxins, petrochemicals, radioactive material and heavy metals in our system, which the *Bikram Yoga*® postures will mobilize. The need to use essential oils to mitigate the effect of these toxins and prevent re-absorption is only beginning to be *appreciated*, much less *practiced*. Essential oils add a much-needed dimension of empowerment to all the tools here and are *indispensable* to ones quest for Self, wholeness, and well being.

***The Power Tap*™**

Like the other vibrational tools shared here, *the Power Tap*™ is a wonderful stand-alone tool for promoting whole being. Derived from a half-century tradition of clinical practice under practitioners like Roger Callahan, James Durlacher, Jimmy Scott, Gary Graig, Robert Kirby, Evelyn Budd-Michaels, and Brian Foley, *the Power Tap*™ draws on the best aspects of techniques like *Thought Field Therapy, EMDR, Emotional Freedom Technique (EFT)*, and many other methods.

However, unlike other methods of energy-meridian tapping and clearing, *no kinesiology* or other diagnostic techiniques are necessary with *the Power Tap*™, and all tapping is self-applied. Experience shows the *Power Tap*™ to be highly effective compared with other clearing procedures, and yet simpler to learn and apply. Memorize *the Power Tap*™, and you will have it when needed; and then you won't have to *think* about it while trying to apply it, which is difficult when negative emotions are presenting and take the mind away.

For an outline of this *energy-meridian stimulation technique* (with a diagram of tapping points), used as an aid to *The SelfQuesting Approach*™ to healing states of consciousness, see the *Power Tap* under the "Vibrational Tools' menu at *www.selfquesting.com*. Similar to resetting a computer that has gone into a bad software/hardware loop, this technique *resets ones subtle energy* system by stimulating known energy meridians on the body. In so doing, it facilitates a relief, balance, and normalization of the body, mind, emotions, and subtle energy by releasing the expression of trapped consciousness from blocked energy structures that are manifesting 'dis-ease' in the body/mind and life.

The important element in effecting the desired relief in the body/mind is *to hold the problem or difficulty in one's awareness* as much as possible while engaging in the tapping procedure. The more clearly and powerfully the problem's content (physical or emotional pain, memory, thought, imagery, etc.) is held in awareness during the tapping sequences, the more quickly and powerfully the problem is resolved. This technique can be applied in combination with essential oils (applied on the tapping fingers and/or points) and used for physical and emotional difficulties or any issue that one would like to explore. The *Power Tap*™ is an excellent tool for opening and exploring the unconscious, and for getting to the deeper *cause* behind the symptoms, including trapped, fragmented awareness (the deepest cause).

Extremely disabling, longstanding problems (phobias, emotional and physical pains, anxiety, depression, addiction, etc.) have been cleared in minutes using *the Power Tap*™ procedure. Don't underestimate its power. Set your intent and apply it with conviction, and you *will* get results. It might require applying the *Power Tap*™ on a problem several times a day for a few weeks, but persist and you will get amazing results that cross over into other areas of your life and being.

If you're stuck, call *the SelfQuesting Center for Whole Being.* Experience shows that a helpful pointer can go a long way in providing the desired relief. If the process fails to bring *permanent* relief, then a more *direct approach* in addressing the trapped consciousness might be required. *The SelfQuesting Approach*™ is as *direct as it gets* in addressing consciousness on its own level, that of *awareness.*

From Personal Experience

Along with essential oils and the Power Tap, *Holosync®* allowed me to step up my Yoga practice from 2-3 days a week to *daily*, without my body breaking down as it had. The synergistic effect of *Young Living Essential Oils®*, *Holosync®*, *the Chi Machine®*, and *Bikram Yoga® or Kali Ray Yoga®* is truly an amazing thing to experience! What the combined use of these tools within the *SelfQuesting*™ process allows for, in terms of opening one to a far greater potential for individual and collective consciousness, will inspire you and place you in awe—an awe of a newfound *potential for life,* and you in it! Old rules, ideas, ways, institutions no longer apply… as one becomes *OneSelf*!

You'll find using the *Chi Machine*® in combination with *YLEO essential oils* during the "*Dive*" track of *Holosync* will greatly ease and accelerate the integration of the *Holosync* program, just as they do the *SelfQuesting*™ work. You'll also find that using these tools reduces addictive cravings and lends an ease to accepting the raw food diet. What these tools will bring to every aspect of your life will amaze you!

Finally, in using these tools you'll want to learn from others. ***A little knowledge from experience can take you a long way. But keep in mind that you are a unique individual with your own needs and path. Be patient. Do not compare yourself with others, and stay out of the ego. Instead focus on doing the best you can for yourself at any time. It's a process – two steps forward, one back – just keep taking those steps. Be the tortoise, not the hare, and you will reach your goal of well-being. Trust in your life's path, and your Self!***

Challenges will present themselves as *fragments* of your undiscovered Self surface, *fearing* change and at the same time *seeking* unity and its power. When you fall out of your commitment to yourself, come back, as you're ready. Stay focused on your (as not yet fully formulated or known) goal of wholeness. You are like the flower blooming in the field—it *knows* not what it's doing, but somehow it blooms. Trust!

You are doing this *for yourself.* Be good to yourself. "Follow your bliss." Apply *the Power Tap*™, and bring persistent difficulties and challenges into your *SelfQuesting*™ sessions. ***If you do this, you'll be amazed at how even***

longstanding issues melt away – issues that you hammered away at for decades with other approaches. Persist and you will soon see growth. Happiness, meaning, and success will reward you in ways you never imagined. And the Love and Oneness of all Being will come to shine through your heart and light your way.

Additional Mind-Body Supports

Along with yoga, the *Five Tibetan Rites* are a set of five (six if you're celibate), brief but effective exercises that optimize time and effort, and give benefits that other exercises don't (see *The Ancient Secret of the Fountain of Youth* by Peter Kepler for instructions).

Additionally, five minutes bouncing or running on a *rebounder* (a small circular trampoline) is *very* effective in moving lymph, trimming fat, building tone, and shaping muscle. As an addition, small handheld weights can be used while "jogging" on the rebounder and making a wide range of arm movements (warm up first and warm down after, by doing the rebounder movements *without* the weights). After WWII, the US Air Force did extensive studies of various forms of exercise, and found use of the rebounder to be an *optimal* exercise with minimal negative impact. A large *exercise ball* (on which the body is *rolled or bounced*) has also been shown to be very beneficial low-impact exercise (as well as serving as a great *desk chair!)*.

A *walk/run,* done on level ground (running only for *very short* periods until the breathing is labored, then walking until the energy and breath return) is excellent aerobic exercise for most people (who are able to run at least minimally), and one for which noticeable benefits can also usually be quickly seen.

Caution: Don't *push* it! Our modern-day conditioning has made it far too easy to overstress and do too much! You *never* have to push, punish, or stress yourself to receive maximum benefit from exercise. ***The "no pain, no gain" approach is an effective program for compromised health, depleted oxygen and vitality, and an early death, but it is not necessary (in fact counterproductive) for success in any useful endeavor.*** Go slowly, and stop or slow down when it is no longer easy, flowing, and stress-free. As an old poster used to say, "Go slowly, it is only yourself to which you have to go." Avoid the *ego* of exercise; discover *the liberation of the Self*

With this approach you'll find exercise (like most things) will be far easier psychologically and physically, and that your overall energy, physical development, and health will more noticeably and quickly improve. Adopt the "Tao" of doing, by doing things when they are *easy* and natural. You'd be surprised how much more you'll accomplish and how much better you'll feel. ***Abandon the obsessive-compulsive sadomasochism of the Modern Age! Enjoy life and <u>being</u>!***

Things to Avoid

In our high-tech material-focused age, many subtle, but important things have been neglected or wrongly created in bringing products to us. Some general precautions and simple measures can make a big difference to our immune system, energy, and health.

When using a *cell phone*, use a low-radiation earpiece/microphone, to move the phone and its radiation away from your body and head (directional antennas might also be useful).

Many new environmental *toxins* have entered our air, water, and food in the last few decades. Stay away from *unnaturally fluoridated* products, including tap water, which are usually tainted with heavy metals that accompany the fluoride. Flouride itself is controversial, having shown to be problematic in numerous clinical studies as well as by its *use* in humans. Politics, greed, and faulty, manipulated research (as seen with nicotine, mercury fillings, aspartame, etc., etc.) have made this the complex issue that it is today. Our governments and the American Medical and Dental Associations are a big part of the problem, having become heavily influenced by vested interests and being unwilling to admit a mistake. Also *avoid chlorinated pools and tap water*, which are especially toxic to the thyroid and endocrine system (and thus the body/mind as a whole) by using a good filter at your water taps (or better yet a whole-house water filter) to remove contaminants.

Refuse silver-mercury fillings and other dental products made with metals. Insist on non-bioactive materials in your mouth, and, if your dentist refuses, go to one of the many and growing number of dentists who have realized the danger of placing these substances in the mouth. Consider replacing your old mercury fillings and dental fixtures with products made from nontoxic porcelain materials (read *It's All in Your Head* by Dr. Hal Huggins). Various essential oils have been clinically documented to *remove* (not just *mobilize*!) heavy metals from the body—use them! Young Living has specific products and protocols that serve this purpose of chelating heavy-metal toxins from the body.

Avoid artificial sweeteners, especially *aspartame* (also known as Nutrisweet, Equal, etc); they appear in soft drinks and thousands of foods and are a serious threat to your health (politics and greed created this crisis in American health – see www.holisticmed.com). Instead use "stevia"—a long-used, safe, natural sweetener that is highly beneficial for those suffering blood-sugar problems, especially diabetics.

Avoid MSG (also called "monosodium glutamate, calcium or sodium casenate, hydroloyzed vegetable or plant protein, textured protein, monopotasium glutamate, autolyzed yeast or yeast extract, glutamic acid," etc), processed sugar, caffeine, and nicotine products for health reasons. Their self-medicating effects deplete awareness and well being. Avoid processed table salt (which has an added "whitener"); instead use unprocessed *sea salt* (also clinically proven to be beneficial).

Other Helps and Hints

Cleanse the liver and gall bladder frequently, using the many methods available. (See the book *Inner Transformations Using Essential Oils* by LeAnne and David Deardeuff, available through Essential Science Publishing, www.essentialscience.net). Chronic fatigue, cold/flu, and many degenerative dis-eases, including cancer, begin with a toxic liver and a "stoned" gall bladder, so don't neglect them. Essential oils of geranium, lavender, juniper, German chamomile, and the Young Living "*Juva*" product line can be very helpful in this process of detoxifying (especially the liver). New products are constantly being introduced by *Young Living* to aid detoxification (for more see *www.youngliving.com/SelfQuest*).

An early-morning drink of fresh-squeezed lemon juice with water, a pinch of cayenne, and stevia is an excellent *charge and cleanse* for the liver, gall bladder, and bowels, setting up the right environment in the intestines. It settles the stomach and clears the sinuses and mind nicely, too.

And don't forget the Chi Machine for cleansing these organs, as well as the lymph. *Nothing* compares with this passive aerobic exerciser's ability to move lymph—less is more.

Balance the hormonal levels and cleanse the hormonal receptor sites. Essential oils, especially those holding *phenol* compounds (such as oils of peppermint, citrus, lavender, and conifers) are very good for unblocking the body's hormone receptor sites of petrochemical and other toxins.

Man or woman, tune up your hormones with a *natural pregnenolone* hormone cream (a precursor to progesterone and estrogen), such as *Young Living's Prenolone, Prenolone+* (with DHEA) and *Regenolone* products, which also contain essential oils to assist this purpose. Essential oils of myrrh, sandalwood, sage, and particularly *clary sage,* can especially be helpful for balancing hormonal levels. Various *Young Living* oil blends and supplements, infused with essential oils, have been created for this purpose. Remember, source and confirmed quality (using gas chromatography / mass spectroscopy / NMR) is everything!

Use essential oils daily that are beneficial and balancing to the mind and emotions, such as frankincense, sandalwood, cedarwood, juniper, lavender, or Young Living essential oil blends such as *Peace and Calming, Valor*, and many others. Discover your own favorites!

Regarding suggestions for essential oils use or an experience of *Young Living Essential Oils* in or out of the *SelfQuesting* process, contact *the SelfQuesting Center for Whole Being*™. We can help you with essential oils use in-person or through phone sessions. We can also explain how you can use oils at home for optimal well-being. See our websites at *www.selfquesting.com* or *www.youngliving.com/SelfQuest*.

(The *Essential Oils Desk Reference* from Essential Science Publishing, 800-336-6308, is a very useful learning tool and ongoing source of info. This book and many other useful titles can be ordered at *www.essentialscience.net*.)

6

Tapping into the power of consciousness, nature's chemistry, and the causal vibrational body

Energy Supports and the Power Tap

The recommendations given previously here involved mostly *Young Living Essentail Oils*. Another very important body-mind support tool that operates powerfully on levels of subtle energy and consciousness, is *the Power Tap* . This technique developed as a *simplified hybrid* and *significant extension* of numerous techniques (such as Roger Callahan's *Thought Field Therapy,* Gary Craig's *Emotional Freedom Technique (EFT), EMDR, Neuro-Emotional Technique, Emotional Complex Clearing,* and many others). Unlike most of these techniques, the *Power Tap* involves no use of complicated procedures such as kinesiology ("muscle testing"), nor does it require the practitioner to touch the client (the client applies the tapping to themselves). *The Power Tap* simply involves the straightforward tapping of one's acupuncture meridian points while mentally holding the problem issue or difficulty in awareness.

The *Power Tap* was developed to provide *everyone* (not just healers and therapists) with a tool for self-empowerment and relief from suffering. Users of this technique have experienced phenomenal shifts in mental, physical, and behavioral debility that years of therapy or drugs did not affect. ***The astoundingly powerful and quick results of the Power Tap method are***

deserving of attention from healers and sufferers alike, especially since with little or no coaching one can apply this technique, on themselves or others, as needed. (We are indebted to the vision and persistence of Brian Foley, MA [Harvard] for being a primary impetus in the creation of these meridian-tapping methods which he calls "*Emotional Mastery Technique.*")

The *Power Tap* method of tapping (and/or applying essential oils or other vibrational products) on acupuncture meridian points of the body, while holding a negative issue (fear, anxiety, panic, phobia, depression, sadness, grief, trauma, overload, loss, addiction, compulsion, memory, physical pain, etc.) in awareness, very powerfully moves to clear the vibrational field of blocks or imbalances that structure dis-ease into the body/mind. In this way, *the Power Tap* relieves suffering of all kinds, durations, causes, and intensities. ***A few minutes of the Power Tap procedure has alleviated suffering that years of therapy and medical expense could not.***

As noted with essential oils, the *Power Tap* can often also be called on to aid in the discovery, release, or integration of fragments of the Self during *SelfQuesting*, and greatly facilitates the ease and speed of the process, as well as the integration of wholeness into the body/mind—even allowing a unification of Self where none would have been possible without this procedure. Sometimes just the *Power Tap* alone can precipitate a release and integration of fragments of the client's Self, thus resulting in a *permanent, global shift* on all levels of their system, requiring no further conscious or other processing.

However, as with essential oils and other vibrational tools, the *Power Tap* should not be used as a shortcut to *force a premature release* of symptoms of a fragment that is presenting for *SelfQuesting* work. To do so can derail the necessary *conscious* processing, resulting in a temporary loss of an opportunity to apply the mental effort required to permanently resolve the deeper *cause* of the problem (trapped consciousness) that *underlies* the vibrational infrastructure. In this case (treating symptoms rather than source), the fragmented Self is delayed or prevented from releasing into wholeness and from integrating that oneness of conscious being into wellness, and so suffering is prolonged.

Further Recommendations

The recommendations made here are part of an overall support program for the body/mind, as well as one's energy and consciousness, while undertaking *the SelfQuesting Approach*, but they are also *generally recommended* supports. Attempts have been made here to give enough information (links) so that sources of products could be located (please mention that *Dr. Greg Hitter* is referring you when you contact these sources). **For more information on *the SelfQuesting Approach*, the *Power Tap*, or on the recommendations made, as well as on the sessions and workshops that Dr. Hitter and his colleagues offer, please contact *SelfQuest* at the phone, address, or email listed at the back of this book.** You will gladly and without obligation be supplied with the information and contacts you need, as well as given a free *SelfQuesting* consultation and assessment if you so desire (also see *www.selfquesting.com*).

A certain amount of common sense needs to be applied in terms of *SelfQuesting*. There are times when a medical doctor (MD) is the necessary choice, and one needs to recognize and appreciate when that is. When one is lying in a hospital emergency ward with a perforated ulcer, this is not a time to engage in *SelfQuesting* —a process that should have been undertaken long before physical imbalances appeared requiring allopathic intervention. When *choosing* a physician, it is recommended this be done (if possible) before such an emergency, and that an MD trained and practiced in *the least-invasive methods* be chosen. ***Contact the American College for the Advancement of Medicine (ACAM, 800-532-3688) for a list of naturally and nutritionally-oriented allopathic physicians ("MD's") in your area (or see their website).*** Establish a relationship with one of these practitioners *before* you need them, and they'll be *available* when you do.

When using any kind of healer, no matter what level of your system their method focuses on (body, mind, energy, consciousness, life), it's recommended that you select a practitioner who appreciates how these various levels interact with each other, and who also importantly appreciates the roll of *consciousness*, in its fragmentation or wholeness, in fundamentally creating dis-ease and life difficulties. Healers of all varieties today appreciate the role of the *mind* (one's thoughts, feelings, and imagery) in the creation of dis-ease, and engage their clients to deal with repressed thoughts and feelings. There is a growing number of healers who also understand the deep role that *subtle energy* plays in causing imbalances to manifest in the mind/body.

Yet many of these healers do not fully understand the deeper role of *consciousness*—as a fundamental cause of dis-ease and difficulty—beyond their fragmented notions of modern science or so-called "spiritual" (religious) traditions. These healers can't see the *limits* of their approach's ability to heal, within the framework of an expanded, enlightened view of consciousness. Nor can they place their view or practice into the context of an approach that brings one's Self into wholeness *in a full and grounded way*, thus promoting truly "holistic," deep, and permanent wellness. In cases where consciousness might be more completely understood and applied, then most often the method of application is limited to *how* the approach engages consciousness, and is also limited in terms of the practitioner's ability to grasp and apply a method that is a *fully-engaged,* consciousness-based approach, unrestrained by the practitioner's own fragmented being and knowing.

An example of this kind of *limited implementation of consciousness* can be seen in chiropractic practices that go beyond just manipulating the body, such as *Network Chiropractic* or Scott Walker's *Neuro-Emotional Technique (NET)*, or the many psychotherapeutic methods (or other healing modalities that focus on elements of the *mind*), or *EMDR, RET, Emotional Complex Clearing*, or the many other *Callahan-type* energy-meridian tapping techniques, which often involve holding the problem in consciousness as a necessary part of the healing (even *the Power Tap* is limited in this way). Again, in general, these methods (when they involve consciousness at all) bring elements of the mind (feelings, thoughts, imagery, memory, etc.) and/or the body (physical sensations of pain) into awareness and hold that dis-ease or difficulty *in awareness* as an important part of the release process.

In some cases, the shifts created by these methods can go so far as to cause a release of fragmented consciousness, thus contributing to an *optimal* shift toward wellness for the client. However, *generally this is not so*, and often these practitioners have *no notion* of the postmodern, enlightened paradigm of bringing the Self into wholeness, nor do they implement an approach that is focused on *directly finding* the fragmented Self that is associated with the problem at hand and *releasing* that trapped awareness back into the consciousness radiating in the body/mind.

Likewise, processes that involve *religious or spiritual methods* of healing and coming into unity, expanding consciousness, freeing energy, and healing the body/mind—to include those that would come under the general description of "spirit releasement," "soul retrieval," "depossession," or the variety of shamanistic or ceremonial forms of magic (including High Ceremonial Magic, which aims to offer a direct experience of the "Higher or Christed" Self [the Self in its wholeness])—usually *do not* display a consciousness-based, *postmodern* understanding (or language) of the *full* human potential. Nor are they able to affect the wholeness and mind/body wellness that an expanded, truly postmodern approach can deliver, particularly in terms of freeing and empowering the individual to live fulfilled, and fully *in the world.*

"Our remedies oft in ourselves do lie, which we ascribe to Heaven."

—William Shakespeare—

The Limits of Hypnotic Suggestion

Since methods have been mentioned that some label "non-suggestive or non-directive" hypnosis (such as "*spirit releasement*"), I will comment briefly on hypnosis in general. Many involved in hypnosis focus their approach on *suggestions* to the mind, believing that *all* healing is 'suggestion,' and thus also that *all* healing can be *reduced* to being seen as suggestive hypnosis. In their mind this form of *reductionism* includes *the SelfQuesting Approach*. But in reducing wellness to notions of *suggestion*, what is missed is the essence and importance of *consciousness* and an approach that aims to find and unite the Self. This limits one's understanding and the power of one's practice and effect.

To believe that healing can be reduced to hypnotic suggestion, is like the athlete who believes that all sports can be reduced to "breathing." Breath and breathing is important in sports (and in healing), but such a focus on breath does not an athlete make. Nor is hypnotic suggestion sufficient to bring wholeness to the Self and create total wellness. Suggestions to the mind operate on the level of *mind*, and do not necessarily involve the specific *conscious processing* needed to liberate trapped awareness. The important "material" in a process of becoming self-aware comes *from the client*, and is not *suggested* by the facilitator. Furthermore, the process of *SelfQuesting* is not driven by *content*—

not the content of the client's thoughts, emotions, memories, sensations, nor the content (however suggestive) of the facilitator's directions.

Instead, *the SelfQuesting Approach* is driven by *the process of awakening awareness alone*; this is the *only* necessary element. Yes, suggestion has the power to effect a relief of mind/body symptoms and even effect a release of fragmented consciousness. And though all kinds of things *might* be suggested in an approach to whole and heal the Self, still *hypnotic suggestion* is not generally sufficient to un-structure the Self into wholeness. Hypnosis can't generally resolve the fundamental energetic infrastructure of *dis-ease* that prevents wellness—the *calling-card* presented by the splintered Self when our lost, trapped awareness uses dis-ease to get our attention *in order to reunite with us.*

It is to the credit of organized hypnosis that it has been able to expand its practice beyond its defined focus of making *suggestions* to the unconscious mind, by accepting "non-directive, non-suggestive" forms of hypnotherapy that attempt to integrate scientific and religious views. Hypnotism's acceptance that important healing elements exist beyond a reductionism to *suggestion,* is healthy and demonstrates the power of enlightened, consciousness-based views to influence movements or institutions beyond their defined boundaries and beyond the limits of their practice, so as to be empowered by these expanded views. We see attempts at this expansion within institutions everywhere today. We also see counter-reactions to these attempts, as institutions and instituted methods and views, reflecting the psyche of the individuals involved, resist the "abnormality" (Thomas Kuhn) and change brought on by the breakdown of old views and an expansion into the postmodern, enlightened era.

"Communication across the revolutionary divide is inevitably partial."

—Thomas Kuhn, The History of Scientific Revolutions—

Summarizing How Vibrational Tools Heal

In recognizing subtle levels of energy and consciousness in human beings, and understanding how these subtle, "butterfly" levels powerfully interrelate with and direct the body/mind, the enlightened *postmodern paradigm* illuminates a pathway by which essential oils, as a vibrational tool, can assist in bring about well-being. Applying this enlightened world-view has expanded *scientific understanding*, to describe *how* essential oils vibrationally affect the body and mind through their influence on one's subtle energy fields and consciousness. And this explains *why* essential oils have been effectively used in so many ways, for so many differing purposes, for millennia. We can also see why essential oils are ever more useful today, as we begin to apply approaches to bringing wholeness to the Self that appreciate the effects of these subtler levels of energy and consciousness on our body, mind, and life, as we apply oils in the light and empowered intent of this new understanding.

Because essential oils, like consciousness, produce *subtle energy vibrations* (emit "light"), essential oils affect the body and mind as they *illuminate* the DNA and RNA in the nucleus of each cell. By the qualities of their *illumination* essential oils are able to effect a vibrational *restructuring* of DNA/RNA "cell memory," and alter the negative *infrastructure of dis-ease* as it effects each cell and the body-mind. By affecting DNA/RNA in this vibrational way--beyond mere biochemistry—oils not only fundamentally determine what happens in the cells and tissues of the body, but also alter how the mind is affected in turn by the biochemistry of the body, and how a person's conscious being can be physically and vibrationally supported toward wholeness using essential oils.

Perhaps the most important role of essential oils as vibrational tools is their profound ability to assist in the *un-structuring* of our fragmented consciousness, to *uncork the fragmented Self bottled in the unconscious.* Oneness of conscious being, as the most subtle but powerful butterfly-level of our being, can then integrate down through the living, energy fields of our system that structure dis-ease. ***So, in their ability to vibrationally counter and balance morphogenic fields of vibrating energy that structure dis-ease, essential oils facilitate mind/body wellness and assist Self-realization and fulfillment by aiding to uncork the 'butterflies' that are our fragmented consciousness and that vibrationally direct our body/mind and life.***

Thus, the *primary pathway* by which essential oils affect changes in the body, mind, energy, and awareness of an individual is now understood by applying a new, enlightened, postmodern world-view that includes but transcends the limits of the two great previous world-views of faith-based religion (the feminine principle, yin) and reason-based science (the masculine principle, yang). Empowered with this *new vision*, our intuitive nature can sense new choices and recognize how to apply what is known, and take specific action to become whole. Thus the enlightened paradigm brings an *intuitive* knowing of how and when essential oils can best be used in the quest to discover and unify the Self.

This paradigm allows for understanding *why* essential oils have had a long history of use in such a wide range of applications in religious practices and healing, and why they are still being used today for these and other purposes. It also explains *how* essential oils are able to influence—through their subtle, but powerful effects—the vibrational infrastructure of human existence—which pre-modern religious and modern scientific views haven't been able to (and often by their design can't) *fully* grasp or illuminate.

New understandings brought by enlightened views of the Self have led to an expansion of essential oil use, beyond mere *chemistry*, into ever-subtler, vibrational, *intuitive* approaches that explore realms of consciousness and wholeness. It is this vibrational "butterfly effect" of essential oils and consciousness to powerfully transform our bodies, minds, and lives which justifies them being called "***butterflies in a bottle***."

"Like the silkworm you have built a cocoon around yourself...
Who will save you?... Burst your own cocoon and come out
as the beautiful butterfly, as the free soul."

—Swami Vivekananda—

Author's Concluding Note

Most of us today really don't fathom how beautiful, sensitive, multi-dimensional, and powerful we are as human beings. Even those who've studied science, medicine, art, literature and religion for a lifetime, struggle to unify into a comprehendible whole the variety of things about ourselves that these differing disciplines describe. Still we undertake this quest to learn, to know ourselves and our world, in order to fully grasp what we as human beings are, what we are capable of, and why we are here.

Modern science tells us one thing about ourselves. Art and literature often bring our awareness to something else. And religion and the spiritual traditions often go in yet another direction. In the confusion we each in unique ways, as we are able, try to integrate these differing ways of knowing in order to comprehend ourselves. Thus is born a personal search for unity, understanding, meaning, and joy—that we know is there to be found, even as we struggle at times through great difficulty and a deep sense of separation. The resulting alienation runs to and from the very core of our being.

Our modern dilemma has been this sense of separation created and perpetuated in part by the fragmented and varying images we hold of ourselves. In presenting an understanding of how essential oils as vibrational tools are able to assist in bringing the body/mind into wholeness, this writing presents an alternate world-view, a vision of hope—hope for a reconciliation of the differing views of science and religion, but more importantly a reconciliation of the divisions within ourselves, toward a Unity beyond mere Truth, to Beauty.

It is the nature of essential oils to render Truth through an experience of Beauty, and the Beauty of their experience extends well beyond their aroma. To be able to receive these truths we must endeavor to be open; open to the lesson, open to ourselves, open to Beauty. It is in this sacred Quest, the act of opening to OneSelf—a radiant state of unified, self-aware being—where the adventure of the learning experience begins, where its path and means are discovered, and where the journey ultimately will end—to return home to OneSelf and truly "know the place for the first time."

Greg Hitter, PhD

For information on workshops and private sessions contact:

The SelfQuesting Center for Whole Being
206 Loma Bonita Drive
San Luis Obispo, CA 93401
(888) 326-8994 toll-free in USA
(805) 781-0309
(Sessions available also by phone)

Email: SelfQuesting@cs.com
Website: www.SelfQuesting.com